THE BRONTË SISTERS

A COLLECTION OF ESSAYS,
EXCERPTS AND WRITINGS ON
THE FAMOUS FEMALE AUTHORS

By

G. K. CHESTERTON,
MRS GASKELL,
VIRGINIA WOOLF,
MRS OLIPHANT AND OTHERS

CONTENTS

BIOGRAPHICAL NOTICE
OF ELLIS AND ACTON BELL

BY CHARLOTTE BRONTË

It has been thought that all the works published under the names of Currer, Ellis, and Acton Bell were, in reality, the production of one person. This mistake I endeavoured to rectify by a few words of disclaimer prefixed to the third edition of 'Jane Eyre.' These, too, it appears, failed to gain general credence, and now, on the occasion of a reprint of 'Wuthering Heights' and 'Agnes Grey,' I am advised distinctly to state how the case really stands.

Indeed, I feel myself that it is time the obscurity attending those two names - Ellis and Acton - was done away. The little mystery, which formerly yielded some harmless pleasure, has lost its interest; circumstances are changed. It becomes, then, my duty to explain briefly the origin and authorship of the books written by Currer, Ellis, and Acton Bell.

About five years ago, my two sisters and myself, after a somewhat prolonged period of separation, found ourselves reunited, and at home. Resident in a remote district, where education had made little progress, and where, consequently, there was no inducement to seek social intercourse beyond our own domestic circle, we were wholly dependent on ourselves and each other, on books and study, for the enjoyments and occupations of life. The highest stimulus, as well as the liveliest pleasure we had known from childhood upwards, lay in attempts at literary composition; formerly we used to show each other what we wrote, but of late years this habit of communication and consultation had been discontinued; hence it ensued, that we were mutually ignorant of the progress we might respectively have made.

One day, in the autumn of 1845, I accidentally lighted on a MS. volume of verse in my sister Emily's handwriting. Of course, I was not surprised, knowing that she could and did write verse: I looked it over, and something more than surprise seized me - a deep conviction that these were not common effusions, nor at all like the poetry women generally write. I thought them condensed and terse, vigorous and genuine. To my ear they had also a peculiar music - wild, melancholy, and elevating.

My sister Emily was not a person of demonstrative character, nor one on the recesses of whose mind and feelings even those nearest and dearest to her could, with impunity, intrude unlicensed; it took hours to reconcile her to the discovery I had made, and days to persuade her that such poems merited publication. I knew, however, that a mind like hers could not be without some latent spark of honourable ambition, and refused to be discouraged in my attempts to fan that spark to flame.

Meantime, my younger sister quietly produced some of her own compositions, intimating that, since Emily's had given me pleasure, I might like to look at hers. I could not but be a partial judge, yet I thought that these verses, too, had a sweet, sincere pathos of their own.

We had very early cherished the dream of one day becoming authors. This dream, never relinquished even when distance divided and absorbing tasks occupied us, now suddenly acquired strength and consistency: it took the character of a resolve. We agreed to arrange a small selection of our poems, and, if possible, to get them printed. Averse to personal publicity, we veiled our own names under those of Currer, Ellis, and Acton Bell; the ambiguous choice being dictated by a sort of conscientious scruple at assuming Christian names positively masculine, while we did not like to declare ourselves women, because - without at that time suspecting that our mode of writing and thinking was not what is called 'feminine' - we had a vague impression that authoresses are liable to be looked on with prejudice; we had noticed how critics sometimes use for their chastisement the weapon of personality, and for their reward, a flattery, which is not true praise.

The bringing out of our little book was hard work. As was to be expected, neither we nor our poems were at all wanted; but for this we had been prepared at the outset; though inexperienced ourselves, we had read the experience of others. The great puzzle lay in the difficulty of getting answers of any kind from the publishers to whom we applied. Being greatly harassed by this obstacle, I ventured to apply to the Messrs. Chambers, of Edinburgh, for a word of advice; *they* may have forgotten the circumstance, but *I* have not, for from them I received a brief and business-like, but civil and sensible reply, on which we acted, and at last made a way.

The book was printed: it is scarcely known, and all of it that merits to be known are the poems of Ellis Bell. The fixed conviction I held, and hold, of the worth of these poems has not indeed received the confirmation of much favourable criticism; but I must retain it notwithstanding.

Ill-success failed to crush us: the mere effort to succeed had given a wonderful zest to existence; it must be pursued. We each set to work on a prose tale: Ellis Bell produced 'Wuthering Heights,' Acton Bell 'Agnes Grey,' and Currer Bell also wrote a narrative in one volume. These MSS. were perseveringly obtruded upon various publishers for the space of a year and a half; usually, their fate was an ignominious and abrupt dismissal.

At last 'Wuthering Heights' and 'Agnes Grey' were accepted on terms somewhat impoverishing to the two authors; Currer Bell's book found acceptance nowhere, nor any acknowledgment of merit, so that something like the chill of despair began to invade her heart. As a forlorn hope, she tried one publishing house more - Messrs. Smith, Elder and Co. Ere long, in a much shorter space than that on which experience had taught her to calculate - there came a letter, which she opened in the dreary expectation of finding two hard, hopeless lines, intimating that Messrs. Smith, Elder and Co. 'were not disposed to publish the MS.,' and, instead, she took out of the envelope a letter of two pages. She read it trembling. It declined, indeed, to publish that tale, for business reasons, but it discussed its merits and demerits so courteously, so considerately, in a spirit so rational, with a discrimination so enlightened, that this very refusal cheered the author better than a vulgarly expressed acceptance would have done. It was added, that a work in three volumes would meet with careful attention.

I was then just completing 'Jane Eyre,' at which I had been working while the one-volume tale was plodding its weary round in London: in three weeks I sent it off; friendly and skilful hands took it in. This was in the commencement of September, 1847; it came out before the close of October following, while 'Wuthering Heights' and 'Agnes Grey,' my sisters' works, which had already been in the press for months, still lingered under a different management.

They appeared at last. Critics failed to do them justice. The immature but very real powers revealed in 'Wuthering Heights' were scarcely recognised; its import and nature were misunderstood; the identity of its author was misrepresented; it was said that this was an earlier and ruder attempt of the same pen which had produced 'Jane Eyre.' Unjust and grievous error! We laughed at it at first, but I deeply lament it now. Hence, I fear, arose a prejudice against the book. That writer who could attempt to palm off an inferior and immature production under cover of one successful effort, must indeed be unduly eager after the secondary and sordid result of authorship, and pitiably indifferent to its true and honourable meed. If reviewers and the public truly believed this, no wonder that they looked darkly on the cheat.

Yet I must not be understood to make these things subject for reproach or complaint; I dare not do so; respect for my sister's memory forbids me. By her any such querulous manifestation would have been regarded as an unworthy and offensive weakness.

It is my duty, as well as my pleasure, to acknowledge one exception to the general rule of criticism. One writer, endowed with the keen vision and fine sympathies of genius, has discerned the real nature of 'Wuthering Heights,' and has, with equal accuracy, noted its beauties and touched on its faults. Too often do reviewers remind us of the mob of Astrologers, Chaldeans, and Soothsayers gathered before the 'writing on the wall,' and unable to read the characters or make known the interpretation. We have a right to rejoice when a true seer comes at last, some man in whom is an excellent spirit, to whom have been given light, wisdom, and understanding; who can accurately read the 'Mene, Mene, Tekel, Upharsin' of an original mind (however unripe, however inefficiently cultured and partially expanded that mind may be); and who can say with confidence, 'This is the interpretation thereof.

Yet even the writer to whom I allude shares the mistake about the authorship, and does me the injustice to suppose that there was equivoque in my former rejection of this honour (as an honour I regard it). May I assure him that I would scorn in this and in every other case to deal in equivoque; I believe language to have been given us to make our meaning clear, and not to wrap it in dishonest doubt?

'The Tenant of Wildfell Hall,' by Acton Bell, had likewise an unfavourable reception. At this I cannot wonder. The choice of subject was an entire mistake. Nothing less congruous with the writer's nature could be conceived. The motives which dictated this choice were pure, but, I think, slightly morbid. She had, in the course of her life, been called on to contemplate, near at hand, and for a long time, the terrible effects of talents misused and faculties abused: hers was naturally a sensitive, reserved, and dejected nature; what she saw sank very deeply into her mind; it did her harm. She brooded over it till she believed it to be a duty to reproduce every detail (of course with fictitious characters, incidents, and situations), as a warning to others. She hated her work, but would pursue it. When reasoned with on the subject, she regarded such reasonings as a temptation to self-indulgence. She must be honest; she must not varnish, soften, nor conceal. This well-meant resolution brought on her misconstruction, and some abuse, which she bore, as it was her custom to bear whatever was unpleasant, with mild, steady patience. She was a very sincere, and practical Christian, but the tinge of religious melancholy communicated a sad shade to her brief, blameless life.

Neither Ellis nor Acton allowed herself for one moment to sink under want of encouragement; energy nerved the one, and endurance upheld the other. They were both prepared to try again; I would fain think that hope and the sense of power were yet strong within them. But a great change approached; affliction came in that shape which to anticipate is dread; to look back on, grief. In the very heat and burden of the day, the labourers failed over their work.

My sister Emily first declined. The details of her illness are deep-branded in my memory, but to dwell on them, either in thought or narrative, is not in my power. Never in all her life had she lingered over any task that lay before her, and she did not linger now. She sank rapidly. She made haste to leave us. Yet, while physically she perished, mentally she grew stronger than we had yet known her. Day by day, when I saw with what a front she met suffering, I looked on her with an anguish of wonder and love. I have seen nothing like it; but, indeed, I have never seen her parallel in anything. Stronger than a man, simpler than a child, her nature stood alone. The awful point was, that while full of ruth for others, on herself she had no pity; the spirit was inexorable to the flesh; from the trembling hand, the unnerved limbs, the faded eyes, the same service was exacted as they had rendered in health. To stand by and witness this, and not dare to remonstrate, was a pain no words can render.

Two cruel months of hope and fear passed painfully by, and the day came at last when the terrors and pains of death were to be undergone by this treasure, which had grown dearer and dearer to our hearts as it wasted before our eyes. Towards the decline of that day, we had nothing of Emily but her mortal remains as consumption left them. She died December 19, 1848.

We thought this enough: but we were utterly and presumptuously wrong. She was not buried ere Anne fell ill. She had not been committed to the grave a fortnight, before we received distinct intimation that it was necessary to prepare our minds to see the younger sister go after the elder. Accordingly, she followed in the same path with slower step, and with a patience that equalled the other's fortitude. I have said that she was religious, and it was by leaning on those Christian doctrines in which she firmly believed, that she found support through her most painful journey. I witnessed their efficacy in her latest hour and greatest trial, and must bear my testimony to the calm triumph with which they brought her through. She died May 28, 1849.

What more shall I say about them? I cannot and need not say much more. In externals, they were two unobtrusive women; a perfectly secluded life gave them retiring manners and habits. In Emily's nature the extremes of vigour and simplicity seemed to meet. Under an unsophisticated culture, inartificial tastes, and an unpretending outside, lay a secret power and fire that might have informed the brain and kindled the veins of a hero; but she had no worldly wisdom; her powers were unadapted to the practical business of life; she would fail to defend her most manifest rights, to consult her most legitimate advantage. An interpreter ought always to have stood between her and the world. Her will was not very flexible, and it generally opposed her interest. Her temper was magnanimous, but warm and sudden; her spirit altogether unbending.

Anne's character was milder and more subdued; she wanted

the power, the fire, the originality of her sister, but was well endowed with quiet virtues of her own. Long-suffering, self-denying, reflective, and intelligent, a constitutional reserve and taciturnity placed and kept her in the shade, and covered her mind, and especially her feelings, with a sort of nun-like veil, which was rarely lifted. Neither Emily nor Anne was learned; they had no thought of filling their pitchers at the well-spring of other minds; they always wrote from the impulse of nature, the dictates of intuition, and from such stores of observation as their limited experience had enabled them to amass. I may sum up all by saying, that for strangers they were nothing, for superficial observers less than nothing; but for those who had known them all their lives in the intimacy of close relationship, they were genuinely good and truly great.

This notice has been written because I felt it a sacred duty to wipe the dust off their gravestones, and leave their dear names free from soil.

AN EXCERPT FROM
Charlotte Bronte's Notes on
the Pseudonyms Used, 1850

ON THE DEATH
OF ANNE BRONTË

A POEM BY CHARLOTTE BRONTË

There's little joy in life for me,
    And little terror in the grave;
I 've lived the parting hour to see
    Of one I would have died to save.

Calmly to watch the failing breath,
    Wishing each sigh might be the last;
Longing to see the shade of death
    O'er those belovèd features cast.

The cloud, the stillness that must part
    The darling of my life from me;
And then to thank God from my heart,
    To thank Him well and fervently;

Although I knew that we had lost
    The hope and glory of our life;
And now, benighted, tempest-tossed,
    Must bear alone the weary strife.

CHARLOTTE BRONTË

BY HATTIE TYNG GRISWOLD

In the crowded little churchyard at Haworth, in the wild, bleak Yorkshire region, are eight mounds which mark the extinction of a family whose genius and sorrows have made them known the world over. In the little church there is a mural tablet which tells the names of this illustrious group, and the many visitors to this little out-of-the-way house of worship read with a melancholy interest these sad inscriptions. First we are told of Maria Bronté, the mother, who died in 1821, when only thirty-nine years old, leaving the six children whose names follow, all in the helplessness of early childhood. Next to her come Maria and Elizabeth, both of whom followed her in 1825; then Branwell and Emily, who died in 1848, and Anne, who lived one year longer. But it is to the last of the inscriptions that all eyes are turned with the greatest interest, for there we read—

CHARLOTTE,
Wife of the Rev. Arthur Bell Nichols, A. B.
and Daughter of the Rev. E. P. Bronté, A. M., Incumbent.
She died March 31st, 1855, in the 39th year of her age.

There is no sadder history in all literature than the history of this gifted family and their early doom. A pathos clings about it which is really painful, so few are the gleams of light which are thrown upon the dark picture. From the time when the Rev. Patrick Bronté (himself a gifted but somewhat erratic man) brought his young wife into the solitude of this moorland parsonage and shut her up in a seclusion from which she was only removed by death, all the way down through the lonely childhood of the little motherless children, and on into their no less lonely and more afflicted womanhood, even to the deaths of all the gifted group, there is a depth of sombre gloom from which the sympathetic heart must turn away with a bitter pain and almost a feeling of hot rebellion against Fate.

The utter loneliness of that part of Yorkshire at the time when Mr. Brontë settled there can hardly be imagined to-day. In winter all communication with the outside world was cut off by almost impassable mud or entirely impassable snow. Travellers whom actual necessity compelled to start forth were often snowed in for a week or ten days within a few miles of home, and nobody thought of stirring from that shelter except through the pressure of absolute necessity. Isolated as were the little hill villages like Haworth, they were in the world, compared with the loneliness of the gray ancestral houses to be seen here and there in the dense hollows of the moors.

The inhabitants of this rough country were themselves of wild, turbulent nature, much given to deadly feuds and really dangerous in their enmities. Their amusements were all of the lowest order, and hard riding and deep drinking were the characteristics of all the male population, while cock-fighting and bull-baiting were thought refined amusements for both sexes.

The ministers were not much above their flocks in general culture, and the incumbents of Haworth had been noted for their eccentricities for generations. Many of them attended the horse-racings and the games of football which were played on Sunday afternoons, and took as deep a part as any of the flock in the drunken carouse which always followed a funeral. Mr. Brontë was a very different man from his predecessors, but was many years in subduing his congregation to an even nominal observance of common moralities. He was, however, a man of high spirit and imperious will, and, bending himself to the task with all his powers, made a decided impression upon the life around him. The gentle mother soon passed away, and Mr. Brontë became a stern and silent man who kept his children at a distance from himself and allowed them little intercourse with the outside world. They were allowed to walk out on the wild heathery moors, but not down in the village street; and they acquired a passionate love of those purple moors, which remained with them through life. When angry, Mr. Brontë would say nothing, but they could hear him out at the door firing pistol-shots in quick succession as a relief to his feelings. The children were unnaturally quiet and well-behaved. The old nurse says:—

"You would never have known there was a child in the house, they were such noiseless, good little creatures. I used to think them spiritless, they were so different from any children I had ever seen."

They used to read the newspapers, write little stories, and act plays, and at one time conducted a magazine of their own. Like all imaginative children, they played in stories, each one taking part in the stirring romances they invented. They were great believers in the supernatural, too, and the denizens of the adjoining churchyard played quite a prominent part in their childish lives. This churchyard, which was so near the parsonage, added much to the gloom and unhealthiness of the old manse, and many people have attributed the ill health of all the girls to its close proximity. It was depressing, to say the least, to such imaginative children as those of Mr. Brontë.

It was not long after the mother's death that the two older girls, Maria and Elizabeth, were taken to a school at Cowan's Bridge, a small hamlet in the north of England, and the younger children were left more lonely than ever. This school, which had been selected on account of its cheapness, had been established for the daughters of clergymen, and the entire expenses were fourteen pounds a year. Cowan's Bridge is prettily situated, just where the Leck-fells sweep into the plain; and by the course of the beck, alders and willows and hazel bushes grow. This little shallow, sparkling stream runs through long green pastures, and has many little falls over beds of gray rocks. The school-house had been made from an old bobbin-mill, and the situation proved to be remarkably unhealthy. This is the school so realistically described by Charlotte in "Jane Eyre." "Helen Burns" is an exact transcript of Maria Bronté, and every scene is a literal description of events which took place at this school. The whole thing was burned into Charlotte's memory so indelibly that she reproduced it with photographic exactness. Emily and Charlotte had followed the other sisters there, after a year or two, so that all of them suffered to a greater or less extent from the privations and abuses they underwent in that female Dotheboys Hall. The eldest sister died, and the second became very ill; yet still Mr. Bronté, who believed in the hardening process for children, kept them there until the health of each one failed in turn, and they were permanently injured by their privations. The food, which would perhaps have been wholesome enough if properly cooked, was ruined by a dirty and careless woman, who served it up in such disgusting messes that many a time the fastidious little Brontés could not eat a mouthful, though faint with hunger. There was always the most delicate cleanliness in the frugal Bronté household, and the children had early learned to be dainty in such matters. Their fare at home was of the simplest nature, but always well cooked; and they simply fasted themselves ill at Cowan's Bridge because they could not eat what was set before them.

There was another trial of health to the girls, and that was being obliged in all kinds of weather to attend church, which was two miles away. The road was a very bleak and unsheltered one, where cutting winds blew in winter and where the snows were often deep. The church was never warmed, as there was no provision made for any heating apparatus; and when the ill-fed and half-clothed girls had reached its shelter, they were often in actual chills from the exposure, and could not hope to gain any additional warmth there. Colds were taken in this way, from which the girls never recovered. They also suffered from cold in the school itself, and from the tyranny of one of the teachers, whom Charlotte has mercilessly depicted as Miss Scatcherd in "Jane Eyre." To the day of Miss Brontë's death, she would blaze with indignation at any mention of this school; and who can wonder?

After the death of the second daughter, Elizabeth, Charlotte and Emily were taken from Cowan's Bridge, and spent some time at another school, where they were much happier, and where they made a few life-long friends, particularly Miss Woolner, the principal. One of her schoolmates gives this description of Charlotte's arrival at the school:—

"I first saw her coming out of a covered cart, in very old-fashioned clothes, and looking very cold and miserable. When she appeared in the school-room her dress was changed, but just as old. She looked a little old woman, so short-sighted that she always appeared to be seeking something, and moving her head from side to side to catch a sight of it. She was very shy and nervous, and spoke with a strong Irish accent. When a book was given her she dropped her head over it till her nose nearly touched it; and when she was told to hold her head up, up went the book after it, still close to her nose, so that it was not possible to help laughing."

She was a close student here, and a favorite with the girls, whom she would frighten half out of their senses by her wonderful stories. So great was their effect at times, that her listeners were thrown into real hysterics. After leaving this school, Charlotte returned home, and began keeping house and teaching her sisters. Here several quiet years were passed, busy but monotonous. The girls spent their time in study, in household tasks, walking, and drawing, of which they were very fond. They also read very thoroughly the few books which were accessible to them. At nineteen Charlotte went as a teacher to Miss Woolner's school, where she was very happy, and remained until her health failed. It was a nervous trouble, which seemed at one time like a complete breaking down, but from which she gradually recovered after her return home. Emily now took her turn in teaching, going to a school at Halifax, where she came near literally dying from homesickness. Emily could never live away from Haworth and her moors; and in this school she labored incessantly from six in the morning till eleven at night, with only one half-hour for exercise between. To a free, wild, untamable spirit like Emily's, this was indeed slavery. She returned home after a time, and Charlotte again went out to teach. They felt the necessity of earning money, as their father's stipend was small, and he was both liberal and charitable,—and there was their brother Branwell to be provided for. Of this brother we have not before spoken; but he occupied an important place in their home and in their lives. He had been the pride and the hope of the family from early youth. He was possessed of brilliant talents, and was full of noble impulses, but was very fond of pleasure, and soon formed irregular habits, which were the ruin of his life and the source of unmeasured grief to his whole family. They had desired to send him to study at the Royal Academy, as he had the family's fondness for drawing, and they fancied he would develop great talent as an artist. Had his habits been good, their hopes might have been realized; but he fell so early into profligacy, that the idea of becoming an artist was given up, and he took a place as a private tutor. He had formed his intemperate habits when a mere boy, at the public house in Haworth village, where he was esteemed royal company,—as no doubt he was, with his brilliant conversational powers,—and was often sent for to entertain chance guests, in whom he delighted, as they could tell him so much of that distant world beyond the confining hills, for which he yearned. The pity of it was infinite; for had he been kept in regular courses for a few years longer, his own ambition and love of the good opinion of others might have restrained him altogether from excess. As it was, before his judgment was matured or he had any real knowledge of the fatal effect of the habits he was forming, he was firmly fixed in the chains of a degrading habit from which death alone could free him. His struggles with this fatal fascination, and his sufferings, were cruel in the extreme, and inflicted pangs bitterer than death on all who loved him. He was rather weak of will, and had been allowed to grow up self-indulgent, through the over-fondness of his family, who were almost ascetic in their own habits, but could deny him nothing. He had great power of attracting people and of attaching them to him,—a power almost wanting in other members of the family, and which might have been of great advantage to him through life, had he started on the right course. As it was, it only helped to drag him down. He had enough of Irish blood in him to make his manners frank and genial, with a kind of natural gallantry about them. He was generally esteemed handsome. His forehead was massive, his eyes good, his mouth pleasant though somewhat coarse, his hair and complexion sandy. Mrs. Gaskell, in her life of Charlotte Bronté, thus tells of the second great grief he caused his family:—

"Branwell, I have mentioned, had obtained a situation as a private tutor. Full of available talent, a brilliant talker, a good writer, apt at drawing, ready of appreciation, and with a not unhandsome person, he took the fancy of a married woman twenty years older than himself. It is no excuse for him to say that she began the first advances, and 'made love' to him. She was so bold and hardened that she did it in the very presence of her children, fast approaching maturity; and they would threaten her that if she did not grant them such and such indulgences, they would tell their bed-ridden father how she went on with Mr. Bronté. He was so beguiled by this mature and wicked woman that he went home for his holiday reluctantly, stayed there as short a time as possible, perplexing and distressing them all by his extraordinary conduct,—at one time in the highest spirits, at another in deepest depression,—accusing himself of blackest guilt and treachery, without specifying what they were; and altogether evincing an irritability of disposition bordering on insanity. Charlotte and her sister suffered acutely from his mysterious behavior. They began to lose all hope in his future career. He was no longer the family pride; an indistinct dread was creeping over their minds that he might turn out the family disgrace.

"After a time the husband of the woman with whom he had intrigued, died. Branwell had been looking forward to this with guilty hope. After her husband's death his paramour would be free; strange as it seems, the young man still loved her passionately, and now imagined the time had come when they might look forward to being married, and might live together without reproach or blame. She had offered to elope with him; she had written to him perpetually; she had sent him money, twenty pounds at a time,—he remembered the criminal advances she had made; she had braved shame and her children's menaced disclosures for his sake; he thought she must love him; he little knew how bad a depraved woman can be. Her husband had made a will, in which he left her his property solely on the condition that she should never see Branwell Brontë again. At the very time the will was read, she did not know but that he might be on his way to her, having heard of her husband's death. She despatched a servant in hot haste to Haworth. He stopped at the Black Bull, and a messenger was sent to the parsonage for Branwell. He came down to the little inn, and was shut up with the man some time. Then the groom went away, and Branwell was left in the room alone. More than an hour elapsed before sign or sound was heard; then those outside heard a noise like the bleating of a calf, and on opening the door he was found in a kind of fit, succeeding to the stupor of grief which he had fallen into on hearing that he was forbidden by his paramour ever to see her again, as, if he did, she would forfeit her fortune. . . . Let her live and flourish. He died, his pockets filled with her letters, which he carried about his person perpetually in order that he might read them as often as he pleased. He lies dead, and his doom is only known to God's mercy."

But he did not die at once. He lived as an abiding care and sorrow and disgrace to his family for three years. He began taking opium, and drank more than ever. "For some time before his death he had attacks of delirium tremens, of the most frightful character; he slept in his father's room, and he would sometimes declare that either he or his father would be dead before morning." The trembling sisters, sick with fright, watched the night through before the door, in such agony as only loving hearts can feel at the ruin of a loved one. The scenes at the old manse at this time would serve to answer the question so often asked, Where did three lonely women like the Bronté sisters ever form their conceptions of such characters as they depicted? How their pure imaginations could conceive of such beings as Heathcote and the Tenant of Wildfell Hall may perhaps be guessed by those who learn what sort of a man Branwell Bronté had grown to be. But the long agony was over at last, and Branwell found his rest; and the sisters, although they could not but feel the relief of his death, mourned for him with passionate sorrow.

Let us turn to pleasanter glimpses of the life at Haworth, some of them preceding the events of which we have been writing. Charlotte had spent a year or two in Brussels, teaching in a school there, and gaining some of those experiences which she afterwards embodied in her novels. Then she had returned home, and the sisters had talked of establishing a school. None of the famous books had yet been written. To show some of Charlotte's ideas at this time, one or two extracts from her letters may be of interest. She writes in 1840:—

"Do not be over-persuaded to marry a man you can never respect,—I do not say *love*; because I think if you can respect a person before marriage, moderate love at least will come after; and as to intense *passion*, I am convinced that that is no desirable feeling. In the first place it seldom or never meets with a requital; and in the second place, if it did, the feeling would be only temporary; it would last the honeymoon, and then perhaps give place to disgust. Certainly this would be the case on the man's part; and on the woman's—God help her if she be left to love passionately and alone.

"I am tolerably well convinced that I shall never marry at all. Reason tells me so, and I am not so utterly the slave of feeling but that I can *occasionally* hear her voice."

This does not sound much like the woman who could write of Jane Eyre and Rochester; but there were depths of passion in the little woman, probably unsuspected by herself.

Again she writes, in 1845:—

"I know that if women wish to escape the stigma of husband-hunting, they must act and look like marble or clay,—cold, expressionless, bloodless; for every appearance of feeling, of joy, sorrow, friendliness, antipathy, admiration, disgust, are alike construed by the world into an attempt to hook a husband. Never mind! well-meaning women have their own consciences to comfort them, after all. Do not therefore be too much afraid of showing yourself as you are, affectionate and good-hearted; do not harshly repress sentiments and feelings excellent in themselves, because you fear that some puppy may fancy you are letting them come out to fascinate him; do not condemn yourself to live only by halves, because if you showed too much animation some pragmatical thing in breeches might take it into his pate to imagine that you desired to dedicate your life to inanity. Write again soon, for I feel rather fierce and want stroking down."

That the sisters were not without their own perturbations and heart troubles, even in the deep seclusion of their lonely home, may be judged by some extracts from a poem written by Emily, who never confided anything to any friend but her own sombre muse.

> "Cold is the earth, and the deep snow piled above thee,
> Far, far removed, cold in the dreary grave.
> Have I forgot, my only love, to love thee,
> Severed at last by Time's all-severing wave?
>
> "Now, when removed, do my thoughts no longer hover
> Over the mountains on that northern shore,

Resting their wings where heath and fern leaves cover
Thy noble heart forever, evermore?

"Cold in the grave, and fifteen wild Decembers
From these brown hills have melted into spring;
Faithful indeed the love is that remembers
After such years of change and suffering."

That Charlotte had some admirers among her father's curates is well known, and that Mr. Nichols paid court to her eight years previous to the time of her marriage with him. That she was capable of intense and passionate devotion there can be no doubt, but we have no hint as to whom she had lavished it upon, in any of her letters.

She was always extremely sensitive about her personal appearance, considering herself irredeemably ugly, and always thinking that people must be disgusted with her looks. She purposely made her heroine in "Jane Eyre" unattractive, as she felt it an injustice that a woman must always be judged by her looks, and she felt that novelists were somewhat to blame in the matter, as they always made their heroines beautiful in person, however unattractive in mind or character. She was extremely short,—"stunted," as she herself calls it,—never having grown any after the days of her starvation at Cowan's Bridge. She had soft brown hair, and good and expressive eyes, though she was so near-sighted; a large mouth; and a broad, square, somewhat overhanging forehead. Her voice was very sweet, and she was not at all the unattractive person she fancied herself, though by no means beautiful. She was exquisitely neat in her dress, and dainty about her gloves and shoes. She had a keen and delicate touch, and could do any difficult work with her hands, which were the smallest perhaps ever seen upon a grown woman. Her needlework was marvellous, and she was an exquisite housekeeper, attending to the minutest details herself. Her circle of friends and acquaintances was a very narrow one all her life, though after the publication of "Jane Eyre" it of course widened and improved.

Harriet Martineau and Mrs. Gaskell proved themselves warm and enthusiastic friends to Charlotte; and Thackeray, who met her in London, where she visited her publishers, was much pleased with her, and wrote very kindly of her after her death. Sir James and Lady Kay Shuttleworth became much interested in her, and she enjoyed her visits to them in Westmoreland very highly. The Lake country was a revelation to her, though she was somewhat oppressed by seeing it all in company. She writes:—

"If I could only have dropped unseen out of the carriage, and gone away by myself in amongst those grand hills and sweet dales, I should have drunk in the full power of this glorious scenery. In company, this can hardly be."

Again she writes to another:—

"Decidedly I find it does not agree with me to prosecute the search for the picturesque in a carriage. A wagon, a spring-cart, even a post-chaise might do; but a carriage upsets everything. I longed to slip out unseen, and to run away by myself in amongst the hills and dales. Erratic and vagrant instincts tormented me; and these I was obliged to control, or rather suppress, for fear of growing in any degree enthusiastic, and thus drawing attention to 'the lioness,' the authoress."

The fact of her having sprung into sudden fame immediately after she was known as the author of "Jane Eyre"—the most wonderful book of her day—was a matter of great surprise to her, and would doubtless have afforded her very keen pleasure, only that she was so overburdened with home cares and sorrows at that time. Even the sweetness of her literary triumph was embittered by the sadness of the home life. "Jane Eyre" had been written during their worst trials with Branwell, and "Shirley" just after his death and during the illness of Emily and Anne, both works being the product of the very darkest hours of her darkened life. If these works are morbid and unhealthy, as has been asserted, is it any wonder, when we consider what must have been the state of her mind while writing them? She was most devotedly attached to her sisters; indeed, her very life may be said to have been bound up in theirs; and it was peculiarly hard for her to lose them just when success appeared to be at hand, and they might have looked forward to something of happiness during the remainder of their lives. Charlotte gives her own affecting account of Emily's death, which throws some light upon the character of that remarkable woman, as remarkable perhaps as Charlotte herself, although she did not live to do any work as lasting as that of her elder sister. She says:—

"But a great change approached. Affliction came in that shape which to anticipate is dread; to look back on, grief. In the very heat and burden of the day the laborers failed over their work. My sister Emily first declined. . . . Never in all her life had she lingered over any task that lay before her, and she did not linger now. She sank rapidly. She made haste to leave us. Day by day, when I saw with what a front she met suffering, I looked on her with an anguish of wonder and love. I have seen nothing like it; but indeed I have never seen her parallel in anything. Stronger than a man, simpler than a child, her nature stood alone. The awful point was that, while full of ruth for others, on herself she had no pity; the spirit was inexorable to the flesh; from the trembling hands, the unnerved limbs, the fading eyes, the same service was exacted as they had rendered in health. To stand by and witness this, and not dare to remonstrate, was a pain no words can render."

Emily never left the house after Branwell's death. She made no complaint, but her friends could see that she was deadly ill. Yet she would have no doctor, and insisted upon going on with her work as usual. This she did until she was actually dying. Branwell had insisted upon standing up to die; and poor Emily had scarcely consented to lie down, when she was gone. Their will-power in their last agonies was something almost fearful to contemplate. As the old bereaved father and Charlotte and Anne followed the coffin to the grave, Emily's old, fierce, faithful bulldog, to which she had been so much attached, came out and walked beside them. When they returned he lay down by Emily's door, and howled pitifully for many days. Charlotte recurred to this death-scene continually. In one letter she says:—

"I cannot forget Emily's death-day; it becomes a more fixed, a darker, a more frequently recurring idea in my mind than ever. It was very terrible. She was torn, conscious, panting, reluctant, though resolute, out of a happy life. But it will not do to dwell on these things."

Anne Brontë did not long survive her sister, and Charlotte was now alone except that she had the care of her aged father, who was feeble and nearly blind. The awful loneliness of the old house almost crazed her, but she went faithfully to work, and bore up with unheard of fortitude. Two or three solitary years went by, when Mr. Nichols, her father's curate, renewed his suit to Miss Brontë. Mrs. Gaskell tells us that he was one who had known her intimately for years, and was not a man to be attracted by any kind of literary fame. He was a grave, reserved, conscientious man, with strong religious feeling. In silence he had watched and loved her long.

She thus describes the meeting:—

"Instead I heard a tap, and like lightning it flashed upon me what was coming. He entered. He stood before me. What his words were you can imagine; his manner you can hardly realize, nor can I forget it. He made me for the first time feel what it costs a man to declare affection when he doubts response.... The spectacle of one ordinarily so statue-like, thus trembling, stirred, and overcome, gave me a strange shock. I could only entreat him to leave me then, and promise a reply on the morrow."

Mr. Brontë, when consulted, was so displeased with the whole proceeding, and was so weak at this time, that Charlotte, fearing ill consequences to him, gave Mr. Nichols a refusal, whereupon he resigned his curacy and left the country. But a year or two after, seeing that Charlotte was unhappy, and fearing for her health, her father withdrew his opposition; Mr. Nichols was recalled, and the marriage finally took place. Mrs. Gaskell says:—

"She expressed herself as thankful to One who had guided her through much difficulty and much distress and perplexity of mind; and yet she felt what most thoughtful women do, who marry when the first flash of careless youth is over, that there was a strange, half-sad feeling in making announcements of an engagement, for cares and fears come mingled inextricably with hopes. One great relief to her mind at this time was derived from the conviction that her father took a positive pleasure in all the thoughts about and preparations for her wedding. He was anxious that things should be expedited, and much interested in preparations for Mr. Nichols's reception into the household."

Again:—

"The news of the wedding had slipt abroad before the little party came out of the church, and many old and humble friends were there, seeing her look 'like a snowdrop' as they say. Her dress was white embroidered muslin, with a lace mantle, and white bonnet trimmed with green leaves, which perhaps might suggest the resemblance to the pale wintry flower."

Her married love and happiness were of very brief duration; a few short months, and she lay upon the bed from which she would rise no more. Waking for an instant, we are told, "from this stupor of intelligence, she saw her husband's woe-worn face, and caught the sound of some murmured words of prayer that God would spare her. 'Oh,' she whispered forth, 'I am not going to die, am I? He will not separate us, we have been so happy.'" But love or prayer could not stay the hand of death, which had marked all of this family for an early doom, and she passed sweetly away in the arms of her devoted husband. Thank God for the little glimpse of womanly happiness which He gave her at the last, and for the faithful mourner who held her memory so sacred for many years in the old gray manse. Mr. Nichols watched faithfully over the old father in his last days, and only left Haworth when duty held him there no longer, although the place had grown inexpressibly sad to him after his affliction. To the graves of the gifted women who sleep there, pilgrimages are made to this day. The Yorkshire region has changed much; and many now seek its wild heathery moors, not only for its own sake, but for the sake of those who loved and suffered in the little gray parsonage among its bleak hills. Long will the genius which created "Jane Eyre" and "Villette" and "Shirley" delight the world; but the remembrance of the writer's womanly virtues will linger when all these shall have passed away.

AN EXCERPT FROM
Home Life of Great Authors, 1886

CHARLOTTE
AND EMILY BRONTË

BY MILLICENT FAWCETT

In the quiet Yorkshire village of Haworth, on the bleak moorland hillside above Keighley, were born two of the greatest imaginative writers of the present century, Charlotte and Emily Brontë. The wonderful gifts of the Brontë family, the grief and tragedy that overshadowed their lives, and their early deaths, will always cast about their story a peculiarly touching interest. Their father, the Rev. Patrick Brontë, was of Irish birth. He was born in the County Down, of a Protestant family—one that had migrated from the south to the north of Ireland. His character was that which we are more accustomed to associate with Scotland than with Ireland. Resolute, stern, independent, and self-denying, he had the virtues of an old Covenanter rather than the facile graces which so often distinguish those of Celtic blood. His father was a farmer, but Patrick Brontë had no desire to live by agricultural industry. At sixteen years of age he separated himself from his family and opened a school. What amount of success he had in this undertaking does not appear, but it is evident that he had a distinct object in view, namely, to obtain money enough to complete his own education; in this he was successful, for after nine years' labour in instructing others, he entered as a student in St. John's College, Cambridge, remained there four years, obtained the B.A. degree of the University, and was ordained as a clergyman of the Church of England. He kept up no intercourse with his family, and showed no trace of his Irish blood, either in speech or character. He loved and married Miss Branwell, of

Penzance, a lady of much sweetness and refinement. Their six children were destined, through the writings of two of them, to be known wherever the English language is spoken, all over the world. After holding livings in Essex and at Thornton, in Yorkshire, Mr. Brontë was appointed to the Rectory of Haworth, which is now so often visited on account of its association with the authors of *Jane Eyre* and *Wuthering Heights*.

Mrs. Brontë's six children were born in rapid succession, and her naturally delicate constitution was further tried by the constant labour and anxiety involved in providing, on very limited means, for the wants of the little brood. Mrs. Gaskell, in her *Life of Charlotte Brontë*, appears to imply that, more than is even usually the case, the weight of family cares and anxieties fell upon the mother rather than the father. "Mr. Brontë," she says, "was, of course, much engaged in his study, and besides, he was not naturally fond of children, and felt their frequent appearance upon the scene as a drag both on his wife's strength and as an interruption to the comfort of the household." One feels disposed to comment on this by saying that children ought never to be born if either of their parents inclines to regard them "as an interruption to the comfort of the household." To give life and grudge it at the same time is not an attractive combination of qualities. Though not much helped by her husband, Mrs. Brontë was, however, not alone in her domestic cares and duties; the eldest of the "interruptions to the comfort of the household," Maria, was a child of wonderfully precocious intellect and heart. Her remarkable character was described in after years by her sister Charlotte as the Helen Burns of *Jane Eyre*. In her, her mother found a sympathising companion and a helper in her domestic cares. The time was rapidly approaching when the mother's place in the household would be vacant, and when many of its duties and responsibilities would be discharged by Maria.

The little Brontës were from their birth unlike other children. The room dedicated to their use was not, even in their babyhood, called their nursery; it was their "study." Little Maria at seven years old would shut herself up in this study with the newspaper, and be able to converse with her father on all the public events of the day, and instruct the other children as to current politics, and upon the characters of the chief personages of the political world.

Mrs. Brontë died in 1821. Maria was then eight; Elizabeth, seven; Charlotte, five; Patrick Branwell, four; Emily, three; and Anne, one. The little motherless brood were left alone for a year, when an elder sister of their mother came to live at the parsonage, but she does not seem to have had any real influence over them. She taught the girls to stitch and sew, and to become proficient in various domestic arts, but she had no sympathy or communion with them, and their real life was lived quite apart from hers. As soon almost as they could read and write at all, they began to compose plays and act them; they had no society but each other's; this, however, was all-sufficient for them. Their power of invention and imagination was very marked; to the habit of composing stories in their own minds they gave the name of "making out." As soon as the labour of writing became less formidable than it always is to baby fingers, the stories thus "made out" were written down. In fifteen months, when Charlotte was about twelve to thirteen years of age, she wrote twenty-two volumes of manuscript, in the minutest hand, which can hardly be deciphered except with the aid of a magnifying-glass. The Duke of Wellington filled a large place in the minds of the Brontës, and in their romances. Something of what the hero was to them when they were children, Charlotte afterwards put into the mouth of Shirley, the heroine of her novel of that name. After the manner of imaginative children, she not only worshipped her hero from afar, but identified herself with him or with members of his family. The authorship of many of her childish romances and poems is ascribed, in her imagination, to the Marquis of Douro, or Lord Charles Wellesley; and when these "goodly youths" are not introduced as authors they often become the chief personages of the story.

The shadow of death that casts so deep a gloom over the story of the Brontë family, first fell on Maria and Elizabeth, the two elder children. The four girls—Maria, Elizabeth, Charlotte, and Emily—had been sent to a school, which was partly a charitable institution, at Cowan Bridge, in Westmoreland. The living at Haworth parsonage was the reverse of luxurious, but the food and the sanitary arrangements at Cowan Bridge were so bad that the health of the little Brontës was seriously injured by it. The food was repulsive from the want of cleanliness with which it was prepared and placed on the table. The children frequently refused food altogether, though sinking from the want of it, rather than drink the "bingy" milk, and eat unappetising scraps from a dirty larder, and puddings made with water taken from rain-tubs and impregnated with the smell of soot and dust. Besides the faulty domestic arrangements of the school, the discipline was harsh and tyrannical, and one teacher in particular was guilty of conduct towards Maria Brontë that can only be called brutal. Low fever broke out at the school, from which about forty of the pupils suffered, but the Brontës did not take the disease. It was evident that Maria was destined for another fate, that of consumption. She was removed from the school only a few days before her death, and Elizabeth followed her to the grave about six weeks later, in June 1825. Even after this Mr. Brontë's eyes were not opened to the danger his children were in by their treatment at Cowan Bridge, and Charlotte and Emily were still allowed to remain at the school. It soon, however, became evident that they would not be long in following Maria and Elizabeth unless they were removed; and they returned home before the rigours of another winter set in. All the physical and mental tortures she endured at Cowan Bridge, Charlotte afterwards described in the account she gives of "Lowood" in *Jane Eyre*. It is not to be taken that the account of "Lowood" is as strictly an accurate description of Cowan Bridge as Charlotte Brontë would have given if she had been simply writing a history of the school. The facts are, perhaps, magnified by the lurid glow of passion and grief with which she recalled her sisters' sufferings. She was only between nine and ten when she left Cowan Bridge, and in the account she wrote of it twenty years later we see rather the impression that was left on her imagination than a strictly accurate history; but there is no doubt that in her account of Maria Brontë's angelic patience, and the cruel persecution to which she was subjected by one of the teachers, the Lowood of *Jane Eyre* is a perfectly faithful transcript of what took place at Cowan Bridge. Mrs. Gaskell says, "Not a word of that part of *Jane Eyre* but is a literal repetition of scenes between the pupil and the teacher. Those who had been pupils at the same time knew who must have written the book from the force with which Helen Burns's sufferings are described."

After the death of Maria and Elizabeth, the next great sorrow of the Brontë family arose from the career of the only son, Patrick Branwell. He was a handsome boy of exceptional mental powers. He had in particular the gift of brilliant conversation, and there was hardly anything he attempted in the way of talking, writing, or drawing which did not do well. In one of Charlotte's letters she says, "You ask me if I do not think that men are strange beings? I do, indeed. I have often thought so; and I think, too, that the mode of bringing them up is strange; they are not sufficiently guarded from temptation. Girls are protected as if they were something very frail and silly indeed, while boys are turned loose on the world, as if they of all beings in existence were the wisest and least liable to be led astray." Poor Branwell, with his brilliant social qualities, was not sufficiently guarded from temptation. The easiest outlet from the narrow walls of Haworth parsonage was to be found at the little inn of Haworth village. The habit of the place was, when any stranger arrived at the inn, for the host to send for the brilliant boy from the parsonage to amuse the guest. The result will easily be guessed. The guiding principle of Charlotte's character was her inexorable fidelity to duty; her whole nature turned with irresistible force to what was right rather than to what was pleasant. With Branwell the reverse was the case.

Conventional propriety of course strictly guarded Charlotte from the possible dangers of associating with casual strangers at the village inn, although her strong resolute character would not have run a tenth part of the risk of contamination as did that of the weak, pleasure-seeking Branwell. It is needless to dwell on the details of his gradual degradation; the high ideals and hopes of his youth were given up; his character became at once coarse and weak. He was entirely incapable of self-government and of retaining any kind of respectable employment. His intemperance and other vices made the daily life of his sisters at the parsonage a nightmare of horrors. For eight years the young man, whose boyhood his family had watched with so much hope and pride, was a source of shame and anguish to them, all the more keenly felt because it could not be openly avowed. Many who knew the family affirmed that so far as purely intellectual qualities were concerned Branwell was even more eminently distinguished than his sisters; but mere intellect, without moral power to guide it, is as dangerous as a spirited horse without bit or bridle. Branwell was singularly deficient in that moral power in which his sisters were so strong, and his education did nothing to supply this natural deficiency. He died in 1848, at the age of thirty.

Cowan Bridge was not the only experience Charlotte and Emily had of school life. They went for a time to another school at Roe Head, where Charlotte was very happy, and in 1835 she returned to the same school as a teacher. In 1842 Charlotte and Emily went to a school in Brussels, where the former stayed two years, the latter only one. All that Charlotte saw and all the friends she made were afterwards portrayed in her stories. One of her most intimate friends became the Caroline Helstone of *Shirley*; the originals of Rose and Jessie Yorke were also among her schoolfellows at Roe Head. There can be little doubt that M. Paul Emanuel of *Villette* was M. Héger of the Brussels school. Every trivial circumstance of an unusually uneventful life became food for her imagination.

The development of Emily's genius was different. Her love of the moors around Haworth was so intense that it was impossible for her to thrive when she was away from them. It became a fact recognised by all the family that Emily must not be taken away from home. The solitude of the wild, dark moors, and the communing with her own heart, together with the dark tragedy of Branwell's wasted life, were the sole sources of Emily's inspiration. Her poems have a wild, untameable quality in them, and her one romance, *Wuthering Heights*, places her in the first rank among the great imaginative writers of English fiction. There is something terrible in Emily's sternness of character, which she never vented pitilessly on any one but herself. She was deeply reserved, and hardly ever, even to her sisters, spoke of what she felt most intensely. A friend who furnished Mrs. Gaskell with some particulars for her biography, states that on one occasion she mentioned "that some one had asked me what religion I was of (with the view of getting me for a partisan), and that I had said that was between God and me. Emily, who was lying on the hearth-rug, exclaimed, 'That's right.' This was all," adds the friend, "I ever heard Emily say on religious subjects." Emily's love for animals was intense; she was especially devoted to a savage old bull-dog named Keeper, who owned no master but herself. The incident in *Shirley* of the heroine being bitten by a mad dog, and straightway burning the wound herself with a red-hot Italian iron, was true of Emily. Her last illness was a time of terrible agony to Charlotte and Anne, not merely because they saw that she who, Charlotte said, was the thing that seemed nearest to her heart in the world was going to be taken from them, but because Emily's resistance to the inroads of illness was so terrible. She resolutely refused to see a doctor, and she would allow no nursing and no tender helpfulness of any kind. It was evident to her agonised sisters that she was dying, but she maintained her savage reserve, suffering in solitary silence rather than admit her pain and weakness. On the very day of her death she rose as usual, dressed herself, and attempted to carry on her usual employments, and all this with the catching, rattling breath and the glazing eye which told that the hand of Death was actually upon her. Charlotte wrote in this agonising hour, "Moments so dark as these I have never known. I pray for God's support to us all. Hitherto He has granted it." At noon on that day, when it was too late, Emily whispered in gasps, "If you will send for a doctor, I will see him now." A few days later Charlotte wrote, "We are very calm at present. Why should we be otherwise? The anguish of seeing her suffer is over; the spectacle of the pains of death is gone by; the funeral day is past. We feel she is at peace. No need to tremble for the hard frost and the keen wind. Emily does not feel them." The terrible anguish of those last days haunted the surviving sisters like a vision of doom. Nearly six months later Charlotte wrote again that nothing but hope in the life to come had kept her heart from breaking. "I cannot forget," she says, "Emily's death-day; it becomes a more fixed, a darker, a more frequently recurring idea in my mind than ever. It was very terrible. She was torn, conscious, panting, reluctant, though resolute, out of a happy life." Within a very short time the gentle youngest sister Anne also died, and Charlotte was left with her father, the last survivor of the family of six wonderful children who had come to Haworth twenty-nine years before.

In earlier and happier days the habit of the sisters had been, when their aunt went to bed at nine o'clock, to put out the candles and pace up and down the room discussing the plots of their novels, and making plans and projects for their future life. Now Charlotte was left to pace the room alone, with all that had been dearest to her in the world under the church pavement at Haworth and in the old churchyard at Scarborough. But Charlotte was not one to give way to self-indulgent idleness, even in the hour of darkest despair. She was writing *Shirley* at the time of Anne's last illness. After the death of this beloved and only remaining sister, she resumed her task; but those who knew what her private history at the time was, can trace in the pages of the novel what she had gone through. The first chapter she wrote after the death of Anne is called, "The Valley of the Shadow of Death."

The first venture in authorship of the sisters was a volume of poems, to which they each contributed. They imagined, probably with justice, that the world was at that time prejudiced against literary women. Therefore they were careful to conceal, even from their publishers, their real identity. The poems were published as the writings of Currer, Ellis, and Acton Bell.

Jane Eyre was the first of Charlotte's stories which was published, but *The Professor* was the first that was written with a view to publication. The sisters each wrote a story—Charlotte, *The Professor*; Emily, *Wuthering Heights*; and Anne, *Agnes Grey*, and sent them to various publishers. Charlotte was the only one of the three sisters whose manuscript was returned on her hands. But she was not discouraged by the disappointment. Just at this time Mr. Brontë, who had been suffering from cataract, was persuaded by his daughters to go to Manchester for an operation. Charlotte accompanied him, and it was while she was waiting on him, in the long suspense after the operation had been performed, that she began *Jane Eyre*, the book that made her, and ultimately the name of Brontë, famous. Nothing is more striking in Charlotte's personal history than the way in which she reproduced the events and personages of her own circle into her novels. Probably the belief that she was writing anonymously encouraged her in this. Her father's threatened blindness and her own fear of a similar calamity are reflected, as it were, in the blindness of Rochester in *Jane Eyre*. The success of *Jane Eyre* was rapid and complete, and there was much dispute whether its author were a man or a woman. The *Quarterly Review* distinguished itself by the remark that if the author were a woman it was evident "she must be one who for some sufficient reason has long forfeited the society of her sex." Sensitive as Charlotte Brontë was, the coarseness of the insult could not wound her; it could at the utmost be regarded as nothing worse than a trivial annoyance; for when the words reached Charlotte, the grave had not long closed over Branwell's wasted life; Emily was just dead, and it was evident that Anne was dying. The greatness of her grief and the anguish of her loneliness dwarfed to their proper proportions the petty insults that at another time would have caused her acute pain. On the whole she had nothing to complain of in the way her book was received; she suffered no lack of generous appreciation from the real leaders of the literary world. Thackeray and G. H. Lewes, Miss Martineau, and Sidney Dobell were warm in their praise of her work. Charlotte's manner of making her literary fame known to her father was characteristic. The secret of their authorship had been very strictly kept by the sisters; but when the success of *Jane Eyre* was assured, Emily and Anne urged Charlotte that their father ought to be allowed to share the pleasure of knowing that she was the writer of the book. Accordingly one afternoon Charlotte entered her father's study and said, "Papa, I've been writing a book." When Mr. Brontë found that the book was not only written, but printed and published, he exclaimed, "My dear, you've never thought of the expense it will be! It will be almost sure to be a loss, for how can you get a book sold? No one knows you or your name."

"But, papa, I don't think it will be a loss; no more will you, if you will just let me read you a review or two, and tell you more about it." At tea that evening Mr. Brontë exclaimed to his other daughters, "Girls, do you know that Charlotte has been writing a book, and it is much better than likely?"

The pacing up and down of the sisters in the firelight, discussing the plots of their novels, has been already mentioned. Mrs. Gaskell records that Charlotte told her that these discussions seldom had any effect in causing her to change the events in her stories, "so possessed was she with the feeling that she had described reality." This confirms what Mr. Swinburne has said of her strongest characteristic as an author, that she has the power of making the reader feel in every nerve that thus and not otherwise it must have been. It must not, however, be thought that the conversations with her sisters were therefore useless; no doubt they were very stimulating to her imagination, and gave her creations more solid reality than they would otherwise have had.

In 1854 Charlotte Brontë married Mr. Nicholls, an Irish gentleman, who had for eight years been her father's curate. She only lived nine months after her marriage. She was happy in her husband's love, and appreciated his devotion to his parish duties. But the loving admirers of Charlotte Brontë can never feel much enthusiasm for Mr. Nicholls. Mrs. Gaskell states that he was not attracted by her literary fame, but was rather repelled by it; he appears to have used her up remorselessly, in their short married life, in the routine drudgery of parish work. She did not complain; on the contrary, she seemed more than contented to sacrifice everything for him and his work; but she remarks in one of her letters, "I have less time for thinking." Apparently she had none for writing. Surely the husband of a Charlotte Brontë, just as much as the wife of a Wordsworth or a Tennyson, ought to be attracted by literary fame. To be the life partner of one to whom the most precious of Nature's gifts is confided, and to be unappreciative of it and even repelled by it, shows a littleness of nature and essential meanness of soul. A true wife or husband of one of these gifted beings should rather regard herself or himself as responsible to the world for making the conditions of the daily life of their distinguished partners favourable to the development of their genius. But pearls have before now been cast before swine, and one cannot but regret that Charlotte Brontë was married to a man who did not value her place in literature as he ought.

AN EXCERPT FROM
Some Eminent Women of our Times
- Short Biographical Sketches, 1889

CHARLOTTE BRONTË

(1816 - 1855)
BY GASKELL

THE authoress of "Jane Eyre" and other works is, as she calls herself [August 1850], undeveloped then, and more than half a head shorter than I am. Soft brown hair, not very dark; eyes very good and expressive, looking straight and open at you, of the same colour as her hair; a large mouth; the forehead square, broad, and rather overhanging. She has a very sweet voice; rather hesitates in choosing her expressions, but when chosen they seem without an effort admirable, and just befitting the occasion; there is nothing overstrained, but perfectly simple. Her nerves were severely taxed by the effort of going among strangers. On one occasion, though the number of the party could not exceed twelve, she suffered the whole day from acute headache, brought on by apprehension of the evening.

It was now [1853] two or three years since I had witnessed a similar effect produced on her, in anticipation of a quiet evening at a friend's home; and since then she had seen many and various people in London; but the physical sensations produced by shyness were still the same, and on the following day she laboured under severe headache. I had several opportunities of perceiving how this nervousness was ingrained in her constitution, and how acutely she suffered in trying to overcome it. One evening we had, among other guests, two sisters who sung Scotch ballads exquisitely. Miss Brontë had been sitting quiet and constrained, till they began "The Bonnie House of Airlie;" but the effect of that, and "Carlyle Yetts" which followed, was as irresistible as the

41

playing of the piper of Hamelin. The beautiful clear light came into her eyes; her lips quivered with emotion; she forgot herself, rose and crossed the room to the piano, where she asked eagerly for song after song. The sisters begged her to come and see them next morning, when they would sing as long as ever she liked, and she promised gladly and thankfully. But on reaching the house her courage failed. We walked some time up and down the street, she upbraiding herself all the while for her folly, and trying to dwell on the sweet echoes in her memory, rather than on the thought of a third sister who would have to be faced if we went in. But it was of no use; and dreading lest this struggle with herself might bring on one of her trying headaches, I entered at last, and made the best apology I could for her non-appearance.

Much of this nervous dread of encountering strangers I ascribed to the idea of her personal ugliness, which had been strongly impressed upon her imagination early in life, and which she exaggerated to herself in a remarkable manner. "I notice," said she, "that after a stranger has once looked at my face, he is careful not to let his eyes wander to that part of the room again." A more untrue idea never entered into any one's head. Two gentlemen who saw her during this visit, without knowing at the time who she was, were singularly attracted by her appearance; and this feeling of attraction towards a pleasant countenance, sweet voice, and gentle, timid manners, was so strong in one as to conquer a dislike he had previously entertained to her works.

There was another circumstance that came to my knowledge at this period, which told secrets about the finely-strung frame. One night I was on the point of narrating some dismal ghost-story, just before bed-time. She shrank from hearing it, and confessed she was superstitious, and prone at all times to the involuntary recurrence of any thoughts of ominous gloom which might have been suggested to her. She said that in first coming to us, she had found a letter on her dressing-table from a friend in Yorkshire, containing a story which had impressed her vividly ever since; that it mingled with her dreams at night, and made her sleep restless and unrefreshing.

[There was a peculiarity about Charlotte Brontë's death.] Not long after her marriage with the Rev. Mr Nicholls, she was attacked by new sensations of perpetual nausea and ever-recurring faintness. "A wren would have starved on what she ate during these last six weeks." Long days and long nights went by; still the same relentless nausea and faintness, and still borne on in patient trust. About the third week in March [1856], there was a change; a low wandering delirium came on, and in it she begged constantly for food, and even for stimulants; she swallowed eagerly now, but it was too late. Wakening for an instant from this stupor of intelligence, she saw her husband's woe-worn face, and caught the sound of some murmured words of prayer that God would spare her. "Oh," she whispered forth, "I am not going to die, am I? He will not separate us, we have been so happy." Early on Saturday morning, March 31, the solemn tolling of Haworth Church bell spoke forth the fact of her death to the villagers who had known her from a child, and whose hearts shivered within them as they thought of the two sitting together [the father and husband] in the old grey house.

AN EXCERPT FROM
*Women of History Selected from
the Writings of Standard Authors, 1896*

CHARLOTTE BRONTË

BY FREDERIC HARRISON

They who are still youthful in the nineties can hardly understand the thrill which went through us all in the forties upon the appearance of *Jane Eyre*, on the discovery of a new genius and a new style. The reputation of most later writers grew by degrees and by repeated impressions of good work. Trollope, George Eliot, Stevenson, George Meredith, did not conquer the interest of the larger public until after many books and by gradual widening of the judgment of experts. But little Charlotte Brontë, who published but three tales in six years and who died at the age of thirty-eight, bounded into immediate fame—a fame that after nearly fifty years we do not even now find to have been excessive.

And then, there was such personal interest in the writer's self, in her intense individuality, in her strong character; there was so much sympathy with her hard and lonely life; there was such pathos in her family history and the tragedy which threw gloom over her whole life, and cut it off in youth after a few months of happiness. To have lived in poverty, in a remote and wild moorland, almost friendless and in continual struggle against sickness, to have been motherless since the age of five, to have lost four sisters and a brother before she was more than thirty-three, to have been sole survivor of a large household, to have passed a life of continual weakness, toil, and suffering—and then to be cut off after nine months of marriage,—all this touched the sympathies of the world as the private life of few writers touches them. And then the shock of her sudden death came upon us as a personal sorrow. Such genius, such courage, such perseverance, such promise—and yet but three books in all, published at intervals of two and of four years! There was meaning in the somewhat unusual form in which Mrs. Gaskell opens her *Life of Charlotte Brontë*, setting out verbatim in her first chapter the seven memorial inscriptions to the buried family in Haworth Church, and placing on the title-page a vignette of Haworth churchyard with its white tombstones. Charlotte Brontë was a kind of prosaic, most demure and orthodox Shelley in the Victorian literature—with visible genius, an intense personality, unquenchable fire, an early and tragic death. And all this passion in a little prim, shy, delicate, proud Puritan girl!

To this sympathy our great writer, whom she herself called "the first social regenerator of the day," did full justice in that beautiful little piece which he wrote in the *Cornhill Magazine* upon her death and which is the last of the *Roundabout Papers* in the twenty-second volume of Thackeray's collected works. It is called *The Last Sketch*: it is so eloquent, so true, so sympathetic that it deserves to be remembered, and yet after forty years it is too seldom read.

Of the multitude that have read her books, who has not known and deplored the tragedy of her family, her own most sad and untimely fate? Which of her readers has not become her friend? Who that has known her books has not admired the artist's noble English, the burning love of truth, the bravery, the simplicity, the indignation at wrong, the eager sympathy, the pious love and reverence, the passionate honour, so to speak, of the woman? What a story is that of that family of poets in their solitude yonder on the gloomy northern moors!

He goes on to deplore that "the heart newly awakened to love and happiness, and throbbing with maternal hope, had ceased to beat." He speaks of her "trembling little frame, the little hand, the great honest eyes." He speaks of his recollections of her in society, of "the impetuous honesty" which seemed the character of the woman—

45

I fancied an austere little Joan of Arc marching in upon us, and rebuking our easy lives, our easy morals. She gave me the impression of being a very pure, and lofty, and high-minded person. A great and holy reverence of right and truth seemed to be with her always. Such, in our brief interview, she appeared to me. As one thinks of that life so noble, so lonely,—of that passion for truth—of those nights and nights of eager study, swarming fancies, invention, depression, elation, prayer; as one reads the necessarily incomplete, though most touching and admirable history of the heart that throbbed in this one little frame—of this one amongst the myriads of souls that have lived and died on this great earth—this great earth?—this little speck in the infinite universe of God—with what wonder do we think of to-day, with what awe await to-morrow, when that which is now but darkly seen shall be clear!

It is quite natural and right that Thackeray, Mrs. Gaskell, indeed all who have spoken of the author of *Jane Eyre*, should insist primarily on the personality of Charlotte Brontë. It is this intense personality which is the distinctive note of her books. They are not so much tales as imaginary autobiographies. They are not objective presentations of men and women in the world. They are subjective sketches of a Brontë under various conditions, and of the few men and women who occasionally cross the narrow circle of the Brontë world. Of the three stories she published, two are autobiographies, and the third is a fancy portrait of her sister Emily. Charlotte Brontë is herself Jane Eyre and Lucy Snowe, and Emily Brontë is Shirley Keeldar. So in *The Professor*, her earliest but posthumous tale, Frances Henri again is simply a little Swiss Brontë. That story also is told as an autobiography, but, though the narrator is supposed to be one William Crimsworth, it is a woman who speaks, sees, and dreams all through the book. The four tales, which together were the work of eight years, are all variations upon a Brontë and the two Brontë worlds in Yorkshire and Belgium. It is most significant (but quite natural) that Mrs. Gaskell in her *Life of Charlotte Brontë* devotes more than half her book to the story of the family before the publication of *Jane Eyre*. The four tales are not so much romances as artistic and imaginative autobiographies.

To say this is by no means to detract from their rare value. The romances of adventure, of incident, of intrigue, of character, of society, or of humour, depend on a great variety of observation and a multiplicity of contrasts. There is not much of Walter Scott, as a man, in *Ivanhoe* or of Alexander Dumas in the *Trois Mousquetaires*; and Dickens, Thackeray, Trollope, Bulwer, Miss Edgeworth, Stevenson, and Meredith—even Miss Austen and George Eliot—seek to paint men and women whom they conceive and whom we may see and know, and not themselves and their own home circle. But Charlotte Brontë told us her own life, her own feelings, sufferings, pride, joy, and ambition. She bared for us her own inner soul, and all that it had known and desired, and this she did with a noble, pure, simple, but intense truth. There was neither egoism, nor monotony, nor commonplace in it. It was all coloured with native imagination and a sense of true art. There is ample room in Art for these subjective idealisations of even the narrowest world. Shelley's lyrics are intensely self-centred, but no one can find in them either realism or egoism. The field in prose is far more limited, and the risk of becoming tedious and morbid is greater. But a true artist can now and then in prose produce most precious portraits of self and glowing autobiographic fantasies of a noble kind.

And Charlotte Brontë was a true artist. She was also more than this; a brave, sincere, high-minded woman, with a soul, as the great moralist saw, "of impetuous honesty." She was not seduced, or even moved, by her sudden fame. She put aside the prospect of success, money, and social distinction as things which revolted her. She was quite right. With all her genius it was strictly and narrowly limited; she was ignorant of the world to a degree immeasurably below that of any other known writer of fiction; her world was incredibly scanty and barren. She had to spin everything out of her own brain in that cold, still, gruesome

Haworth parsonage. It was impossible for any genius to paint a world of which it was as ignorant as a child. Hence, in eight years she only completed four tales for publication. And she did right. With her strict limits both of brain and of experience she could not go further. Perhaps, as it was, she did more than was needed. *Shirley* and *Villette*, with all their fine scenes, are interesting now mainly because Charlotte Brontë wrote them, and because they throw light upon her brain and nature. *The Professor* is entirely so, and has hardly any other quality. We need not groan that we have no more than we have from her pen. *Jane Eyre* would suffice for many reputations and alone will live.

In considering the gifted Brontë family, it is really Charlotte alone who finally concerns us. Emily Brontë was a wild, original, and striking creature, but her one book is a kind of prose *Kubla Khan*—a nightmare of the superheated imagination. Anne Brontë always seems but a pale reflection of the family. In any other family she might be interesting—just as "Barrel Mirabeau" was the good boy and fool of the Mirabeau family, though in another family he would have been the genius and the profligate. And so, the poems of the whole three are interesting as psychologic studies, but have hardly a single stanza that can be called poetry at all. It is significant, but hardly paradoxical, that Charlotte's verses are the worst of the three. How many born writers of musical prose have persisted in manufacturing verse of a curiously dull and unmelodious quality! The absolute masters of prose and of verse in equal perfection hardly exceed Shakespeare and Shelley, Goethe and Hugo. And Charlotte Brontë is an eminent example of a strong imagination working with freedom in prose, but which began by using the instrument of verse, and used it in a manner that never rose for an instant above mediocrity.

Of the Brontës it is Charlotte only who concerns us, and of Charlotte's work it is *Jane Eyre* only that can be called a masterpiece. To call it a masterpiece, as Thackeray did, is not to deny its manifold and manifest shortcomings. It is a very small corner of the world that it gives, and that world is seen by a single acute observer from without. The plain little governess dominates the whole book and fills every page. Everything and every one appear, not as we see them and know them in the world, but as they look to a keen-eyed girl who had hardly ever left her native village. Had the whole book been cast into the form of impersonal narration, this limitation, this huge ignorance of life, this amateur's attempt to construct a romance by the light of nature instead of observation and study of persons, would have been a failure. As the autobiography of Jane Eyre—let us say at once of Charlotte Brontë—it is consummate art. It produces the illusion we feel in reading *Robinson Crusoe*. In the whole range of modern fiction there are few characters whom we feel that we know so intimately as we do Jane Eyre. She is as intensely familiar to us as Becky Sharp or Parson Adams. Much more than this. Not only do we feel an intimate knowledge of Jane Eyre, but we see every one by the eyes of Jane Eyre only. Edward Rochester has not a few touches of the melodramatic villain; and no man would ever draw a man with such conventional and Byronic extravagances. If Edward Rochester had been described in impersonal narrative with all his brutalities, his stage villain frowns, and his Grand Turk whims, it would have spoiled the book. But Edward Rochester, the "master" of the little governess, as seen by the eyes of a passionate, romantic, but utterly unsophisticated girl, is a powerful character; and all the inconsistencies, the affectation, the savageries we might detect in him, become the natural love-dream of a most imaginative and most ignorant young woman.

A consummate master of style has spoken, we have just seen, of the "noble English" that Charlotte Brontë wrote. It is true that she never reached the exquisite ease, culture, and raciness of Thackeray's English. She lapsed now and then into provincial solecisms; she "named" facts as well as persons; girls talk of a "beautiful man"; nor did she know anything of the scientific elaboration of George Eliot or the subtle grace of Stevenson.

But the style is of high quality and conscientious finish—terse, pure, picturesque, and sound. Like everything she did, it was most scrupulously honest—the result of a sincere and vivid soul, resolved to utter what it had most at heart in the clearest tone. Very few writers of romance have ever been masters of a style so effective, so nervous, so capable of rising into floods of melody and pathos. There is a fine passage of the kind in one of her least-known books, the earliest indeed of all, which no publisher could be found in her lifetime to print. The "Professor" has just proposed, has been accepted, and goes home to bed half-crazy and fasting. A sudden reaction falls on his over-wrought nerves.

A horror of great darkness fell upon me; I felt my chamber invaded by one I had known formerly, but had thought for ever departed. I was temporarily a prey to hypochondria. She had been my acquaintance, nay, my guest, once before in boyhood; I had entertained her at bed and board for a year; for that space of time I had her to myself in secret; she lay with me, she ate with me, she walked out with me, showing me nooks in woods, hollows in hills, where we could sit together, and where she could drop her drear veil over me, and so hide sky and sun, grass and green tree; taking me entirely to her death-cold bosom, and holding me with arms of bone. What tales she would tell me at such hours! What songs she would recite in my ears! How she would discourse to me of her own country—the grave—and again and again promise to conduct me there ere long; and drawing me to the very brink of a black, sullen river, show me, on the other side, shores unequal with mound, monument, and tablet, standing up in a glimmer more hoary than moonlight. "Necropolis!" she would whisper, pointing to the pale piles, and add, "It contains a mansion prepared for you."

Finely imagined—finely said! It has the ring and weird mystery of De Quincey. There are phrases that Thackeray would not have used, such as jar on the ear and betray an immature taste. "Necropolis" is a strange affectation when "City of the Dead" was at hand; and "pointing to the pale piles" is a hideous alliteration. But in spite of such immaturities (and the writer never saw the text in type) the passage shows wonderful power of language and sense of music in prose. How fine is the sentence, "taking me to her death-cold bosom, and holding me with arms of bone," and that of the tombstones, "in a glimmer more hoary than moonlight" Coleridge might have used such a phrase in the *Ancient Mariner* or in *Christabel*. Yet these were the thoughts and the words of a lonely girl of thirty as she watched the dreary churchyard at Haworth from the windows of its unlovely parsonage.

This vivid power of painting in words is specially called forth by the look of nature and the scenes she describes. Charlotte Brontë had, in the highest degree, that which Ruskin has called the "pathetic fallacy," the eye which beholds nature coloured by the light of the inner soul. In this quality she really reaches the level of fine poetry. Her intense sympathy with her native moors and glens is akin to that of Wordsworth. She almost never attempts to describe any scenery with which she is not deeply familiar. But how wonderfully she catches the tone of her own moorland, skies, storm-winds, secluded hall or cottage!

The charm of the hour lay in its approaching dimness, in the low-gliding and pale-beaming sun. I was a mile from Thornfield, in a lane noted for wild roses in summer, for nuts and blackberries in autumn, and even now possessing a few coral treasures in hips and haws, but whose best winter delight lay in its utter solitude and leafless repose. If a breath of air stirred, it made no sound here; for there was not a holly, not an evergreen to rustle, and the stripped hawthorn and hazel bushes were as still as the white worn stones which causewayed the middle of the path. Far and wide, on each side, there were only fields, where no cattle now browsed; and the little brown birds, which stirred occasionally in the hedge, looked like single russet leaves that had forgotten to drop. . . . From my seat I could look down on Thornfield: the gray and battlemented hall was the principal object in the vale below me; its woods and dark rookery rose against the west. I lingered till the sun went down amongst the trees, and sank crimson and clear behind them.

How admirable is this icy hush of nature in breathless expectation of the first coming of the master of Thornfield—of the master of Jane herself. And yet, how simple in phrase, how pure, how Wordsworthian in its sympathy with earth even in her most bare and sober hues! And then that storm which ushers in the story of the Vampyre woman tearing Jane's wedding veil at her bedside, when "the clouds drifted from pole to pole, fast following, mass on mass." And as Jane watches the shivered chestnut-tree, "black and riven, the trunk, split down the centre, gasped ghastly"—a strange but powerful alliteration. "The moon appeared momentarily in that part of the sky which filled the fissure; her disk was blood-red and half overcast; she seemed to throw on me one bewildered, dreary glance, and buried herself again instantly in the deep drift of cloud." An admirable overture to that terrific scene of the mad wife's visit to the rival's bed.

Charlotte Brontë is great in clouds, like a prose Shelley. We all recall that mysterious storm in which *Villette* darkly closes, and with it the expected bridegroom of Lucy Snowe—

The wind takes its autumn moan; but—he is coming. The skies hang full and dark—a rack sails from the west; the clouds cast themselves into strange forms—arches and broad radiations; there rise resplendent mornings—glorious, royal, purple as monarch in his state; the heavens are one flame; so wild are they, they rival battle at its thickest—so bloody, they shame Victory in her pride. . . . When the sun returned his light was night to some!

And into that night Lucy's master, lover, husband has for ever passed.

This sympathy with nature, and this power to invest it with feeling for the human drama of which it is the scene, lifts little Charlotte Brontë into the company of the poets. No one, however, can enter into all the art of her landscapes unless he knows those Yorkshire moors, the straggling upland villages, bare, cold, gray, uncanny, with low, unlovely stone buildings, and stern church towers and graveyards, varied with brawling brooks and wooded glens, and here and there a grim manor-house that had seen war. It is so often that the dwellers in the least picturesque and smiling countries are found to love their native country best and to invest it with the most enduring art. And the pilgrims to Haworth Parsonage have in times past been as ardent as those who flock to Grasmere or to Abbotsford.

Jane Eyre is full of this "pathetic fallacy," or aspect of nature dyed in the human emotions of which it is the mute witness. The storm in the garden at night when Rochester first offers marriage to his little governess, and they return to the house drenched in rain and melted with joy, is a fine example of this power. From first to last, the correspondence between the local scene and the human drama is a distinctive mark in *Jane Eyre*.

If I were asked to choose that scene in the whole tale which impresses itself most on my memory, I should turn to the thirty-sixth chapter when Jane comes back to have a look at Thornfield Hall, peeps on the battlemented mansion which she had loved so well, and is struck dumb to find it burnt out to a mere skeleton—"I looked with timorous joy toward a stately house: I saw a blackened ruin." The suddenness of this shock, its unexpected and yet natural catastrophe, its mysterious imagery of the loves of Edward Rochester and Jane Eyre, and the intense sympathy which earth, wood, rookery, and ruin seem to feel for the girl's eagerness, amazement, and horror, have always seemed to me to reach the highest note of art in romance. It is now forty-seven years since I first read that piece; and in all these years I have found no single scene in later fiction which is so vividly and indelibly burnt into the memory as is this. The whole of this chapter, and what follows it, is intensely real and true. And the very dénoûment of the tale itself—that inevitable bathos into which the romance so often dribbles out its last inglorious breath—has a manliness and sincerity of its own: "the sky is no longer a blank to him—the earth no longer a void."

The famous scene in the twenty-sixth chapter with the

interrupted marriage, when Rochester drags the whole bridal party into the den of his maniacal wife, the wild struggle with the mad woman, the despair of Jane—all this is as powerful as anything whatever in English fiction. It is even a masterpiece of ingenious construction and dramatic action. It is difficult to form a cool estimate of a piece so intense, so vivid, and so artful in its mechanism. The whole incident is conceived with the most perfect reality; the plot is original, startling, and yet not wholly extravagant. But it must be confessed that the plot is not worked out in details in a faultless way. It is undoubtedly in substance "sensational," and has been called the parent of modern sensationalism. Edward Rochester acts as a Rochester might; but he too often talks like the "wicked baronet" of low melodrama. The execution is not always quite equal to the conception. The affiance of Jane and Edward Rochester, their attempted marriage, the wild temptation of Jane, her fierce rebuff of the tempter, his despair and remorse, her agony and flight—all are consummate in conception, marred here and there as they are in details by the blue fire and conventional imprecations of the stage.

The concluding chapters of the book, when Jane finally rejects St. John Rivers and goes back to Thornfield and to her "master," are all indeed excellent. St. John is not successful as a character; but he serves to produce the crisis and to be foil to Rochester. St. John, it is true, is not a real being: like Rochester, he is a type of man as he affects the brain and heart of a highly sensitive and imaginative girl. Objectively speaking, as men living and acting in a practical world, St. John and Rochester are both in some degree caricatures of men; and, if the narrative were a cold story calmly composed by a certain Miss Brontë to amuse us, we could not avoid the sense of unreality in the men. But the intensity of the vision, the realism of every scene, the fierce yet self-governed passion of Jane herself, pouring out, as in a secret diary, her agonies of love, of scorn, of pride, of abandonment,—all this produces an illusion on us: we are no longer reading a novel of society, but we are admitted to the wild musings of a girl's soul;

and, though she makes out her first lover to be a generous brute and her second lover to be a devout machine, we feel it quite natural that Jane, with her pride and her heart of fire and her romantic brain, should so in her diary describe them.

St. John Rivers, if we take him coolly outside of Jane's portrait gallery, is little more than a puppet. We never seem to get nearer to his own mind and heart, and his conduct and language are hardly compatible with the noble attributes with which he is said to be adorned. A man of such refined culture, of such high intelligence, of such social distinction and experience, of such angelic character, does not treat women with studied insolence and diabolical cynicism. That a girl, half maddened by disappointed love, should romantically come to erect his image into that of a sort of diabolic angel, is natural enough, and her conduct when she leaves Moor House is right and true, though we cannot say as much for Rivers' words. But the impression of the whole scene is right.

In the same way, Edward Rochester, if we take him simply as a cultured and travelled country gentleman, who was a magnate and great *parti* in his county, is barely within the range of possibility. As St. John Rivers is a walking contradictory of a diabolic saint, so Edward Rochester is a violent specimen of the heroic ruffian. In Emily Brontë's gruesome phantasmagoria of *Wuthering Heights* there is a ruffian named Heathcliff; and, whatever be his brutalities and imprecations, we always feel in reading it that *Wuthering Heights* is merely a grisly dream, not a novel at all. Edward Rochester has something of the Heathcliff too. But Rochester is a man of the best English society, courted by wealth and rank, a man of cultivated tastes, of wide experience and refined habits, and lastly of most generous and heroic impulses—and yet such a man swears at his people like a horse-dealer, teases and bullies his little governess, treats his adopted child like a dog, almost kicks his brother-in-law in his rages, plays shocking tricks with his governess at night, offers her marriage, and attempts to commit bigamy in his own parish with his living wife still under the same roof! That a man of Rochester's resource, experience, and forethought, should keep his maniac wife in his own ancestral home where he is entertaining the county families and courting a neighbouring peer's sister, and that, after the maniac had often attempted murder and arson—all this is beyond the range of probabilities. And yet the story could not go on without it. And so, Edward Rochester, man of the world as he is, risks his life, his home, and everything and every one dear to him in order that his little governess, Jane Eyre, should have the materials for inditing a thrilling autobiography. It cannot be denied that this is the very essence of "sensationalism," which means a succession of thrilling surprises constructed out of situations that are practically impossible.

Nor, alas! can we deny that there are ugly bits of real coarseness in *Jane Eyre*. It is true that most of them are the effects of that portentous ignorance of the world and of civilised society which the solitary dreamer of Haworth Parsonage had no means of removing. The fine ladies, the lords and soldiers in the drawing-room at Thornfield are described with inimitable life, but they are described as they appeared to the lady's-maids, not to each other or to the world. Charlotte Brontë perhaps did not know that an elegant girl of rank does not in a friend's house address her host's footman before his guests in these words— "Cease that chatter, blockhead! and do my bidding." Nor does a gentleman speak to his governess of the same lady whom he is thought to be about to marry in these terms—"She is a rare one, is she not, Jane? A strapper—a real strapper, Jane: big, brown, and buxom." But all these things are rather the result of pure ignorance. Charlotte Brontë, when she wrote her first book, had hardly ever seen any Englishmen but a few curates, the villagers, and her degraded brother, with rare glimpses of lower middle-class homes. But Jane Eyre's own doings and sayings are hardly the effect of mere ignorance. Her nocturnal adventures with her "master" are given with delightful *naïveté*; her consenting to hear out her "master's" story of his foreign amours is not pleasant. Her two avowals to Edward Rochester—one before he had declared his love for her, and the other on her return to him—are certainly somewhat frank. Jane Eyre in truth does all but propose marriage twice to Edward Rochester; and she is the first to avow her love, even when she believed he was about to marry another woman. It is indeed wrung from her; it is human nature; it is a splendid encounter of passion; and if it be bold in the little woman, it is redeemed by her noble defiance of his tainted suit, and her desperate flight from her married lover.

But Jane Eyre's ignorances and simplicities, the improbabilities of her men, the violence of the plot, the weird romance about her own life, are all made acceptable to us by being shown to us only through the secret visions of a passionate and romantic girl. As the autobiography of a brave and original woman, who bares to us her whole heart without reserve and without fear, *Jane Eyre* stands forth as a great book of the nineteenth century. It stands just in the middle of the century, when men were still under the spell of Byron, Shelley, Coleridge, and Wordsworth, and yet it is not wholly alien to the methods of our latest realists.

It is true that a purely subjective work in prose romance, an autobiographic revelation of a sensitive heart, is not the highest and certainly not the widest art. Scott and Thackeray—even Jane Austen and Maria Edgeworth—paint the world, or part of the world, as it is, crowded with men and women of various characters. Charlotte Brontë painted not the world, hardly a corner of the world, but the very soul of one proud and loving girl. That is enough: we need ask no more. It was done with consummate power. We feel that we know her life, from ill-used childhood to her proud matronhood; we know her home, her school, her professional duties, her loves and hates, her agonies and her joys, with that intense familiarity and certainty of vision with which our own personal memories are graven on our brain. With all its faults, its narrowness of range, its occasional extravagances, *Jane Eyre* will long be remembered as one of the most creative influences of the Victorian literature, one of the most poetic pieces of English romance, and among the most vivid masterpieces in the rare order of literary "Confessions."

AN EXCERPT FROM
Studies in Early Victorian Literature, 1895

CHARLOTTE BRONTË

THE COUNTRY PARSON'S DAUGHTER
BY ASA DON DICKINSON

Mrs. Gaskell's "Life of Charlotte Brontë" is one of the great biographies of literature, but like other works on the same theme, it is really a history of the Brontë family during the period of Charlotte's life. The individuals of this family were for many years as closely associated with one another as they were closely hidden from the outside world. The personality of each was influenced by its house-mates to an unusual degree. They studied each other and they studied every book that came within reach. Themselves they knew well: the world, through books only. This probably accounts for the weird and even morbid character of much of their work. Their vivid imaginations, unchecked by experience, in a commonplace world were allowed free play, and as a result we find some of the most original creations in the whole realm of literature.

The life of the Brontë sisterhood should convince the literary aspirant that the creative imagination is sufficient unto itself and independent of the stimulus of contact with the busy hum of men. If it be necessary, the literary genius by divination can portray life without seeing it. Bricks are produced without straw.

From "Life of Charlotte Brontë," by Mrs. E. C. Gaskell.

But the children did not want society. To small infantine gayeties they were unaccustomed. They were all in all to each other. I do not suppose that there ever was a family more tenderly bound to each other. Maria read the newspapers, and reported intelligence to her younger sisters which it is wonderful they could take an interest in. But I suspect that they had no "children's books," and their eager minds "browsed undisturbed among the wholesome pasturage of English literature," as Charles Lamb expresses it. The servants of the household appear to have been much impressed with the little Brontës' extraordinary cleverness. In a letter which I had from him on this subject, their father writes: "The servants often said they had never seen such a clever little child" (as Charlotte), "and that they were obliged to be on their guard as to what they said and did before her. Yet she and the servants always lived on good terms with each other...."

I return to the father's letter. He says:

"When mere children, as soon as they could read and write, Charlotte and her brothers and sisters used to invent and act little plays of their own in which the Duke of Wellington, my daughter Charlotte's hero, was sure to come off conqueror; when a dispute would not unfrequently arise amongst them regarding the comparative merits of him, Bonaparte, Hannibal, and Caesar. When the argument got warm, and rose to its height, as their mother was then dead, I had sometimes to come in as arbitrator, and settle the dispute according to the best of my judgment. Generally, in the management of these concerns, I frequently thought that I discovered signs of rising talent, which I had seldom or never before seen in any of their age.... A circumstance now occurs to my mind which I may as well mention. When my children were very young, when, as far as I can remember, the oldest was about ten years of age, and the youngest about four, thinking they knew more than I had yet discovered, in order to make them speak with less timidity, I deemed that if they were put under a sort of cover I might gain my end; and happening to have a mask in the house, I told them all to stand and speak boldly from under cover of the mask.

"I began with the youngest (Anne, afterward Acton Bell), and asked what a child like her most wanted; she answered, 'Age and experience.' I asked the next (Emily, afterward Ellis Bell) what I had best do with her brother Branwell, who was sometimes a naughty boy; she answered, 'Reason with him, and when he won't listen to reason, whip him.' I asked Branwell what was the best way of knowing the difference between the intellects of men and women; he answered, 'By considering the difference between them as to their bodies.' I then asked Charlotte what was the best book in the world; she answered, 'The Bible.' And what was the next best; she answered, 'The Book of Nature.' I then asked the next what was the best mode of education for a woman; she answered, 'That which would make her rule her house well.' Lastly I asked the oldest what was the best mode of spending time; she answered, 'By laying it out in preparation for a happy eternity.'

"I may not have given precisely their words, but I have nearly done so, as they made a deep and lasting impression on my memory. The substance, however, was exactly what I have stated."

The strange and quaint simplicity of the mode taken by the father to ascertain the hidden characters of his children, and the tone and character of these questions and answers, show the curious education which was made by the circumstances surrounding the Brontës. They knew no other children. They knew no other modes of thought than what were suggested to them by the fragments of clerical conversation which they overheard in the parlour, or the subjects of village and local interest which they heard discussed in the kitchen. Each had their own strong characteristic flavour.

They took a vivid interest in the public characters, and the local and foreign politics discussed in the newspapers. Long before Maria Brontë died, at the age of eleven, her father used to say he would converse with her on any of the leading topics of the day with as much freedom and pleasure as with any grown-up person....

Miss Branwell instructed the children at regular hours in all she could teach, making her bed-chamber into their schoolroom. Their father was in the habit of relating to them any public news in which he felt an interest; and from the opinions of his strong and independent mind they would gather much food for thought; but I do not know whether he gave them any direct instruction. Charlotte's deep, thoughtful spirit appears to have felt almost painfully the tender responsibility which rested upon her with reference to her remaining sisters. She was only eighteen months older than Emily; but Emily and Anne were simply companions and playmates, while Charlotte was motherly friend and guardian to both; and this loving assumption of duties beyond her years made her feel considerably older than she really was.

I have had a curious packet confided to me, containing an immense amount of manuscript, in an inconceivably small space; tales, dramas, poems, romances, written principally by Charlotte, in a hand which is almost impossible to decipher without the aid of a magnifying glass....

As each volume contains from sixty to a hundred pages ... the amount of the whole seems very great, if we remember that it was all written in about fifteen months. So much for the quantity; the quality strikes me as of singular merit for a girl of thirteen or fourteen. Both as a specimen of her prose style at this time, and also as revealing something of the quiet domestic life led by these children, I take an extract from the introduction to "Tales of the Islanders," the title of one of their "Little Magazines":

"JUNE the 31st, 1829.

"The play of the 'Islanders' was formed in December, 1827, in the following manner: One night, about the time when cold sleet and stormy fogs of November are succeeded by the snowstorms and high, piercing night-winds of confirmed winter, we were all sitting round the warm blazing kitchen fire, having just concluded a quarrel with Tabby concerning the propriety of lighting a candle, from which she came off victorious, no candle having been produced. A long pause succeeded, which was at last broken by Branwell saying in a lazy manner, 'I don't know what to do.' This was echoed by Emily and Anne.

"Tabby. 'Wha ya may go t'bed.'

"Branwell. 'I'd rather do anything than that.'

"Charlotte. 'Why are you so glum to-night, Tabby? Oh! suppose we had each an island of our own.'

"Branwell. 'If we had I would choose the Island of Man.'

"Charlotte. 'And I would choose the Isle of Wight.'

"Emily. 'The Isle of Arran for me.'

"Anne. 'And mine should be Guernsey.'

"We then chose who would be chief men in our Islands. Branwell chose John Bull, Astley Cooper, and Leigh Hunt; Emily, Walter Scott, Mr. Lockhart, Johnny Lockhart; Anne, Michael Sadler, Lord Bentinck, Sir Henry Halford. I chose the Duke of Wellington and two sons, Christopher North and Co., and Mr. Abernethy. Here our conversation was interrupted by the, to us, dismal sound of the clock striking seven, and we were summoned off to bed. The next day we added many others to our list of men, till we got almost all the chief men of the kingdom. After this, for a long time, nothing worth noticing occurred. In June, 1828, we erected a school on a fictitious island, which was to contain 1,000 children. The manner of the building was as follows: The island was fifty miles in circumference, and certainly appeared more like the work of enchantment than anything real," etc....

There is another scrap of paper in this all but illegible handwriting, written about this time, and which gives some idea of the sources of their opinions....

"Papa and Branwell are gone for the newspaper, the Leeds *Intelligencer*, a most excellent Tory newspaper, edited by Mr. Wood, and the proprietor, Mr. Henneman. We take two, and see three, newspapers a week. We take the Leeds *Intelligencer*, Tory, and the Leeds *Mercury*, Whig, edited by Mr. Baines, and his brother, son-in-law, and his two sons, Edward and Talbot. We see the *John Bull*; it is a high Tory, very violent. Mr. Driver lends us it, as likewise *Blackwood's Magazine*, the most able periodical there is. The editor is Mr. Christopher North, an old man seventy-four years of age; the 1st of April is his birthday;

his company are Timothy Tickler, Morgan O'Doherty, Macrabin Mordecai, Mullion, Warnell, and James Hogg, a man of most extraordinary genius, a Scottish shepherd. Our plays were established, 'Young Men,' June, 1826; 'Our Fellows,' July, 1827; 'Islanders,' December, 1827. These are our three great plays that are not kept secret. Emily's and my best plays were established the 1st of December, 1827; the others March, 1828. Best plays mean secret plays, they are very nice ones. All our plays are very strange ones. Their nature I need not write on paper, for I think I shall always remember them. The 'Young Men's' play took its rise from some wooden soldiers Branwell had; 'Our Fellows' from 'Aesop's Fables'; and the 'Islanders' from several events which happened. I will sketch out the origin of our plays more explicitly if I can. First, 'Young Men.' Papa brought Branwell some wooden soldiers at Leeds; when papa came home it was night, and we were in bed, so next morning Branwell came to our door with a box of soldiers. Emily and I jumped out of bed, and I snatched up one and exclaimed, 'This is the Duke of Wellington! This shall be the Duke!' When I had said this Emily likewise took one up and said it should be hers; when Anne came down, she said one should be hers. Mine was the prettiest of the whole, and the tallest, and the most perfect in every part. Emily's was a grave-looking fellow, and we called him 'Gravey.' Anne's was a queer little thing, much like herself, and we called him 'Waiting-boy.' Branwell chose his, and called him 'Buonaparte.'"

The foregoing extract shows something of the kind of reading in which the little Brontës were interested; but their desire for knowledge must have been excited in many directions, for I find a "list of painters whose works I wish to see," drawn up by Charlotte Brontë when she was scarcely thirteen: "Guido Reni, Julio Romano Titian, Raphael, Michael Angelo, Coreggio, Annibal Carracci, Leonardo da Vinci, Fra Bartolomeo, Carlo Cignani, Vandyke, Rubens, Bartolomeo Ramerghi."

Here is this little girl, in a remote Yorkshire parsonage, who has probably never seen anything worthy the name of a painting in her life studying the names and characteristics of the great old Italian and Flemish masters, whose works she longs to see some time, in the dim future that lies before her! There is a paper remaining which contains minute studies of, and criticisms upon, the engravings in "Friendship's Offering for 1829," showing how she had early formed those habits of close observation and patient analysis of cause and effect, which served so well in after-life as handmaids to her genius.

The way in which Mr. Brontë made his children sympathize with him in his great interest in politics must have done much to lift them above the chances of their minds being limited or tainted by petty local gossip. I take the only other remaining personal fragment out of "Tales of the Islanders"; it is a sort of apology, contained in the introduction to the second volume, for their not having been continued before; the writers have been for a long time too busy and lately too much absorbed in politics:

"Parliament was opened, and the great Catholic question was brought forward, and the Duke's measures were disclosed, and all was slander, violence, party spirit, and confusion. Oh, those six months, from the time of the King's speech to the end! Nobody could write, think, or speak on any subject but the Catholic question, and the Duke of Wellington, and Mr. Peel. I remember the day when the *Intelligence Extraordinary* came with Mr. Peel's speech in it, containing the terms on which the Catholics were to be let in! With what eagerness papa tore off the cover, and how we all gathered round him, and with what breathless anxiety we listened, as one by one they were disclosed, and explained, and argued upon so ably and so well; and then when it was all out, how aunt said that she thought it was excellent, and that the Catholics could do no harm with such good security. I remember also the doubts as to whether it would pass the House of Lords, and the prophecies that it would not; and when the paper came which was to decide the question, the anxiety was almost dreadful with which we listened to the whole affair; the opening of the doors, the hush; the royal dukes in their robes, and the great duke in green sash and waistcoat; the rising of all the peeresses when he rose; the reading of his speech—papa saying that his words were like precious gold; and lastly, the majority of one to four (sic) in favour of the Bill. But this is a digression."

This must have been written when she was between thirteen and fourteen.

She was an indefatigable student; constantly reading and learning; with a strong conviction of the necessity and value of education very unusual in a girl of fifteen. She never lost a moment of time, and seemed almost to grudge the necessary leisure for relaxation and play-hours, which might be partly accounted for by the awkwardness in all games occasioned by her shortness of sight. Yet, in spite of these unsociable habits, she was a great favourite with her school-fellows. She was always ready to try and do what they wished, though not sorry when they called her awkward, and left her out of their sports. Then, at night, she was an invaluable story-teller, frightening them almost out of their wits as they lay in bed. On one occasion the effect was such that she was led to scream out loud, and Miss Wooler, coming upstairs, found that one of the listeners had been seized with violent palpitations, in consequence of the excitement produced by Charlotte's story.

Her indefatigable craving for knowledge tempted Miss Wooler on into setting her longer and longer tasks of reading for examination; and toward the end of the two years that she remained as a pupil at Roe Head, she received her first bad mark for an imperfect lesson. She had had a great quantity of Blair's "Lectures on Belles-Lettres" to read; and she could not answer some of the questions upon it; Charlotte Brontë had a bad mark. Miss Wooler was sorry, and regretted that she had over-tasked so willing a pupil. Charlotte cried bitterly. But her school-fellows were more than sorry—they were indignant. They declared that the infliction of ever so slight a punishment on Charlotte Brontë was unjust—for who had tried to do her duty like her?—and testified their feeling in a variety of ways, until Miss Wooler, who was in reality only too willing to pass over her good pupil's first fault, withdrew the bad mark....

After her return home she employed herself in teaching her sisters over whom she had had superior advantages. She writes thus, July 21, 1832, of her course of life at the parsonage:

"An account of one day is an account of all. In the morning, from nine o'clock till half-past twelve, I instruct my sisters, and draw; then we walk till dinner-time. After dinner I sew till tea-time, and after tea I either write, read, or do a little fancywork, or draw, as I please. Thus, in one delightful though somewhat monotonous course, my life is passed. I have been out only twice to tea since I came home. We are expecting company this afternoon, and on Tuesday next we shall have all the female teachers of the Sunday-school to tea."

It was about this time that Mr. Brontë provided his children with a teacher in drawing, who turned out to be a man of considerable talent but very little principle. Although they never attained to anything like proficiency, they took great interest in acquiring this art; evidently from an instinctive desire to express their powerful imaginations in visible forms. Charlotte told me that at this period of her life drawing and walking out with her sisters formed the two great pleasures and relaxations of her day...

Quiet days, occupied in teaching and feminine occupations in the house, did not present much to write about; and Charlotte was naturally driven to criticise books.

Of these there were many in different plights, and according to their plight, kept in different places. The well bound were ranged in the sanctuary of Mr. Brontë's study; but the purchase of books was a necessary luxury to him, and as it was often a choice between binding an old one, or buying a new one, the familiar volume, which had been hungrily read by all the members of the family, was sometimes in such a condition that the bedroom shelf was considered its fitting place. Up and down the house were to be found many standard works of a solid kind. Sir Walter Scott's writings, Wadsworth's and Southey's poems were among the lighter literature; while, as having a character of their own—earnest, wild, and occasionally fanatical, may be named some of the books which came from the Branwell side of the family—from the Cornish followers of the saintly John Wesley—and which are touched on in the account of the works to which Caroline Helstone had access in "Shirley": "Some venerable Lady's Magazines, that had once performed a voyage with their owner, and undergone a storm"—(possibly part of the relics of Mrs. Brontë's possessions, contained in the ship wrecked on the coast of Cornwall)—"and whose pages were stained with salt water; some mad Methodist Magazines full of miracles and apparitions, and preternatural warnings, ominous dreams, and frenzied fanaticism; and the equally mad Letters of Mrs. Elizabeth Rowe from the Dead to the Living."

Mr. Brontë encouraged a taste for reading in his girls; and though Miss Branwell kept it in due bounds by the variety of household occupations, in which she expected them not merely to take a part, but to become proficients, thereby occupying regularly a good portion of every day, they were allowed to get books from the circulating library at Keighley; and many a happy walk up those long four miles must they have had burdened with some new book into which they peeped as they hurried home. Not that the books were what would generally be called new; in the beginning of 1833 the two friends [Charlotte and "E.," a school friend] seem almost simultaneously to have fallen upon "Kenilworth," and Charlotte writes as follows about it:

"I am glad you like 'Kenilworth'; it is certainly more resembling a romance than a novel; in my opinion, one of the most interesting works that ever emanated from the great Sir Walter's pen. Varney is certainly the personification of consummate villainy; and in the delineation of his dark and profoundly and artful mind, Scott exhibits a wonderful knowledge of human nature, as well as surprising skill in embodying his perceptions, so as to enable others to become participators in that knowledge...."

Meanwhile, "The Professor" had met with many refusals from different publishers; some, I have reason to believe, not over-courteously worded in writing to an unknown author, and none alleging any distinct reasons for its rejection. Courtesy is always due; but it is, perhaps, hardly to be expected that, in the press of business in a great publishing house, they should find time to explain why they decline particular works. Yet, though one course of action is not to be wondered at, the opposite may fall upon a grieved and disappointed mind with all the graciousness of dew; and I can well sympathize with the published account which "Currer Bell" gives, of the feelings experienced on reading Messrs. Smith and Elder's letter containing the rejection of "The Professor."

"As a forlorn hope, we tried one publishing house more. Ere long, in a much shorter space than that on which experience had taught him to calculate, there came a letter, which he opened in the dreary anticipation of finding two hard, hopeless lines, intimating that 'Messrs. Smith and Elder were not disposed to publish the MS.,' and, instead, he took out the envelope a letter of two pages. He read it, trembling. It declined, indeed, to publish that tale, for business reasons, but it discussed its merits and demerits so courteously, so considerately, in a spirit so rational, with a discrimination so enlightened, that this very refusal cheered the author better than a vulgarly expressed acceptance would have done. It was added, that a work in three volumes would meet with careful attention."

Mr. Smith has told me a little circumstance connected with the reception of this manuscript which seems to me indicative of no ordinary character. It came (accompanied by the note given below) in a brown paper parcel, to 65 Cornhill. Besides the address to Messrs. Smith & Co., there were on it those of other publishers to whom the tale had been sent, not obliterated, but simply scored through, so that Messrs. Smith at once perceived the names of some of the houses in the trade to which the unlucky parcel had gone, without success.

[*To Messrs. Smith and Elder*]

"JULY 15th, 1847.

"Gentlemen—I beg to submit to your consideration the accompanying manuscript. I should be glad to learn whether it be such as you approve, and would undertake to publish at as early a period as possible. Address, Mr. Currer Bell, under cover to Miss Brontë, Haworth, Bradford, Yorkshire."

Some time elapsed before an answer was returned....

[*To Messrs. Smith and Elder*]

"AUGUST 2nd, 1847.

"Gentlemen—About three weeks since I sent for your consideration a MS. entitled 'The Professor, a Tale by Currer Bell.' I should be glad to know whether it reached your hands safely, and likewise to learn, at your earliest convenience, whether it be such as you can undertake to publish. I am, gentlemen, yours respectfully,

"CURRER BELL.

"I enclose a directed cover for your reply."

This time her note met with a prompt answer; for, four days later, she writes (in reply to the letter she afterward characterized in the Preface to the second edition of "Wuthering Heights," as containing a refusal so delicate, reasonable, and courteous as to be more cheering than some acceptances):

"Your objection to the want of varied interest in the tale is, I am aware, not without grounds; yet it appears to me that it might be published without serious risk, if its appearance were speedily followed up by another work from the same pen, of a more striking and exciting character. The first work might serve as an introduction, and accustom the public to the author's name: the success of the second might thereby be rendered more probable. I have a second narrative in three volumes, now in progress, and nearly completed, to which I have endeavoured to impart a more vivid interest than belongs to 'The Professor.' In about a month I hope to finish it, so that if a publisher were found for 'The Professor' the second narrative might follow as soon as was deemed advisable; and thus the interest of the public (if any interest was aroused) might not be suffered to cool. Will you be kind enough to favour me with your judgment on this plan?"…

Mr. Brontë, too, had his suspicions of something going on; but, never being spoken to, he did not speak on the subject, and consequently his ideas were vague and uncertain, only just prophetic enough to keep him from being actually stunned when, later on, he heard of the success of "Jane Eyre"; to the progress of which we must now return.

[*To Messrs. Smith and Elder*]

"AUGUST 24th.

"I now send you per rail a MS. entitled 'Jane Eyre,' a novel in three volumes, by Currer Bell. I find I cannot prepay the carriage of the parcel, as money for that purpose is not received at the small station-house where it is left. If, when you acknowledge the receipt of the MS., you would have the goodness to mention the amount charged on delivery, I will immediately transmit it in postage stamps. It is better in future to address Mr. Currer Bell, under cover to Miss

Brontë, Haworth, Bradford, Yorkshire, as there is a risk of letters otherwise directed not reaching me at present. To save trouble, I enclose an envelope."

"Jane Eyre" was accepted, and printed and published by October 16th....

When the manuscript of "Jane Eyre" had been received by the future publishers of that remarkable novel, it fell to the share of a gentleman connected with the firm to read it first. He was so powerfully struck by the character of the tale that he reported his impression in very strong terms to Mr. Smith, who appears to have been much amused by the admiration excited. "You seem to have been so enchanted that I do not know how to believe you," he laughingly said. But when a second reader, in the person of a clear-headed Scotchman, not given to enthusiasm, had taken the MS. home in the evening, and became so deeply interested in it as to sit up half the night to finish it, Mr. Smith's curiosity was sufficiently excited to prompt him to read it for himself; and great as were the praises which had been bestowed upon it, he found that they had not exceeded the truth.

AN EXCERPT FROM
Stories of Achievement IV, 1895

ANNE BRONTË

BY CLEMENT K. SHORTER

It can scarcely be doubted that Anne Brontë's two novels, *Agnes Grey* and *The Tenant of Wildfell Hall*, would have long since fallen into oblivion but for the inevitable association with the romances of her two greater sisters. While this may he taken for granted, it is impossible not to feel, even at the distance of half a century, a sense of Anne's personal charm. Gentleness is a word always associated with her by those who knew her. When Mr. Nicholls saw what professed to be a portrait of Anne in a magazine article, he wrote: 'What an awful caricature of the dear, gentle Anne Brontë!' Mr. Nicholls has a portrait of Anne in his possession, drawn by Charlotte, which he pronounces to be an admirable likeness, and this does convey the impression of a sweet and gentle nature.

Anne, as we have seen, was taken in long clothes from Thornton to Haworth. Her godmother was a Miss Outhwaite, a fact I learn from an inscription in Anne's *Book of Common Prayer*. '*Miss Outhwaite to her goddaughter, Anne Brontë, July 13th, 1827.*' Miss Outhwaite was not forgetful of her goddaughter, for by her will she left Anne £200.

There is a sampler worked by Anne, bearing date January 23rd, 1830, and there is a later book than the Prayer Book, with Anne's name in it, and, as might be expected, it is a good-conduct prize. *Prize for good conduct presented to Miss A. Brontë with Miss Wooler's kind love, Roe Head, Dec. 14th,* 1836, is the inscription in a copy of Watt *On the Improvement of the Mind.*

Apart from the correspondence we know little more than

this—that Anne was the least assertive of the three sisters, and that she was more distinctly a general favourite. We have Charlotte's own word for it that even the curates ventured upon 'sheep's eyes' at Anne. We know all too little of her two experiences as governess, first at Blake Hall with Mrs. Ingham, and later at Thorp Green with Mrs. Robinson. The painful episode of Branwell's madness came to disturb her sojourn at the latter place, but long afterwards her old pupils, the Misses Robinson, called to see her at Haworth; and one of them, who became a Mrs. Clapham of Keighley, always retained the most kindly memories of her gentle governess.

With the exception of these two uncomfortable episodes as governess, Anne would seem to have had no experience of the larger world. Even before Anne's death, Charlotte had visited Brussels, London, and Hathersage (in Derbyshire). Anne never, I think, set foot out of her native county, although she was the only one of her family to die away from home. Of her correspondence I have only the two following letters:—

TO MISS ELLEN NUSSEY

'Haworth, *October 4th*, 1847.

'My dear Miss Nussey,—Many thanks to you for your unexpected and welcome epistle. Charlotte is well, and meditates writing to you. Happily for all parties the east wind no longer prevails. During its continuance she complained of its influence as usual. I too suffered from it in some degree, as I always do, more or less; but this time, it brought me no reinforcement of colds and coughs, which is what I dread the most. Emily considers it a very uninteresting wind, but it does not affect her nervous system. Charlotte agrees with me in thinking the—[1] a very provoking affair. You are quite mistaken about her parasol;

she affirms she brought it back, and I can bear witness to the fact, having seen it yesterday in her possession. As for my book, I have no wish to see it again till I see you along with it, and then it will be welcome enough for the sake of the bearer. We are all here much as you left us. I have no news to tell you, except that Mr. Nicholls begged a holiday and went to Ireland three or four weeks ago, and is not expected back till Saturday; but that, I dare say, is no news at all. We were all and severally pleased and gratified for your kind and judiciously selected presents, from papa down to Tabby, or down to myself, perhaps I ought rather to say. The crab-cheese is excellent, and likely to be very useful, but I don't intend to need it. It is not choice but necessity has induced me to choose such a tiny sheet of paper for my letter, having none more suitable at hand; but perhaps it will contain as much as you need wish to read, and I to write, for I find I have nothing more to say, except that your little Tabby must be a charming little creature. That is all, for as Charlotte is writing, or about to write to you herself, I need not send any messages from her. Therefore accept my best love. I must not omit the Major's[2] compliments. And—Believe me to be your affectionate friend,

'ANNE BRONTË.'

Footnotes:

[1] The original of this letter is lost, so that it is not possible to fill in the hiatus.

[2] Emily—who was called the Major, because on one occasion she guarded Miss Nussey from the attentions of Mr. Weightman during an evening walk.

TO MISS ELLEN NUSSEY

'Haworth, *January 4th*, 1848.

'My dear Miss Nussey,—I am not going to give you a "nice *long* letter"—on the contrary, I mean to content myself with a shabby little note, to be ingulfed in a letter of Charlotte's, which will, of course, be infinitely more acceptable to you than any production of mine, though I do not question your friendly regard for me, or the indulgent welcome you would accord to a missive of mine, even without a more agreeable companion to back it; but you must know there is a lamentable deficiency in my organ of language, which makes me almost as bad a hand at writing as talking, unless I have something particular to say. I have now, however, to thank you and your friend for your kind letter and her pretty watch-guards, which I am sure we shall all of us value the more for being the work of her own hands. You do not tell us how *you* bear the present unfavourable weather. We are all cut up by this cruel east wind. Most of us, i.e. Charlotte, Emily, and I have had the influenza, or a bad cold instead, twice over within the space of a few weeks. Papa has had it once. Tabby has escaped it altogether. I have no news to tell you, for we have been nowhere, seen no one, and done nothing (to speak of) since you were here—and yet we contrive to be busy from morning till night. Flossy is fatter than ever, but still active enough to relish a sheep-hunt. I hope you and your circle have been more fortunate in the matter of colds than we have.

'With kind regards to all,—I remain, dear Miss Nussey, yours ever affectionately,

'ANNE BRONTË.'

Agnes Grey, as we have noted, was published by Newby, in

one volume, in 1847. *The Tenant of Wildfell Hall* was issued by the same publisher, in three volumes, in 1848. It is not generally known that *The Tenant of Wildfell Hall* went into a second edition the same year; and I should have pronounced it incredible, were not a copy of the later issue in my possession, that Anne Brontë had actually written a preface to this edition. The fact is entirely ignored in the correspondence. The preface in question makes it quite clear, if any evidence of that were necessary, that Anne had her brother in mind in writing the book. 'I could not be understood to suppose,' she says, 'that the proceedings of the unhappy scapegrace, with his few profligate companions I have here introduced, are a specimen of the common practices of society: the case is an extreme one, as I trusted none would fail to perceive; but I knew that such characters do exist, and if I have warned one rash youth from following in their steps, or prevented one thoughtless girl from falling into the very natural error of my heroine, the book has not been written in vain.' 'One word more and I have done,' she continues. 'Respecting the author's identity, I would have it to be distinctly understood that Acton Bell is neither Currer nor Ellis Bell, and, therefore, let not his faults be attributed to them. As to whether the name is real or fictitious, it cannot greatly signify to those who know him only by his works.'

TO W. S. WILLIAMS

'*January* 18*th*, 1849.

'My dear Sir,—In sitting down to write to you I feel as if I were doing a wrong and a selfish thing. I believe I ought to discontinue my correspondence with you till times change, and the tide of calamity which of late days has set so strongly in against us takes a turn. But the fact is, sometimes I feel it absolutely necessary to unburden my mind. To papa I must only speak cheeringly, to Anne only encouragingly—to you I may give some hint of the dreary truth.

'Anne and I sit alone and in seclusion as you fancy us, but we do not study. Anne cannot study now, she can scarcely read; she occupies Emily's chair; she does not get well. A week ago we sent for a medical man of skill and experience from Leeds to see her. He examined her with the stethoscope. His report I forbear to dwell on for the present—even skilful physicians have often been mistaken in their conjectures.

'My first impulse was to hasten her away to a warmer climate, but this was forbidden: she must not travel; she is not to stir from the house this winter; the temperature of her room is to be kept constantly equal.

'Had leave been given to try change of air and scene, I should hardly have known how to act. I could not possibly leave papa; and when I mentioned his accompanying us, the bare thought distressed him too much to be dwelt upon. Papa is now upwards of seventy years of age; his habits for nearly thirty years have been those of absolute retirement; any change in them is most repugnant to him, and probably could not, at this time especially when the hand of God is so heavy upon his old age, be ventured upon without danger.

'When we lost Emily I thought we had drained the very dregs of our cup of trial, but now when I hear Anne cough as Emily coughed, I tremble lest there should be exquisite bitterness yet to taste. However, I must not look forwards, nor must I look backwards. Too often I feel like one crossing an abyss on a narrow plank—a glance round might quite unnerve.

'So circumstanced, my dear sir, what claim have I on your friendship, what right to the comfort of your letters? My literary character is effaced for the time, and it is by that only you know me. Care of papa and Anne is necessarily my chief present object in life, to the exclusion of all that could give me interest with my publishers or their connections. Should Anne get better, I think I could rally and become Currer Bell once more, but if otherwise, I look no farther: sufficient for the day is the evil thereof.

'Anne is very patient in her illness, as patient as Emily was unflinching. I recall one sister and look at the other with a sort of reverence as well as affection—under the test of suffering neither has faltered.

'All the days of this winter have gone by darkly and heavily like a funeral train. Since September, sickness has not quitted the house. It is strange it did not use to be so, but I suspect now all this has been coming on for years. Unused, any of us, to the possession of robust health, we have not noticed the gradual approaches of decay; we did not know its symptoms: the little cough, the small appetite, the tendency to take cold at every variation of atmosphere have been regarded as things of course. I see them in another light now.

'If you answer this, write to me as you would to a person in an average state of tranquillity and happiness. I want to keep myself as firm and calm as I can. While papa and Anne want me, I hope, I pray, never to fail them. Were I to see you I should endeavour to converse on ordinary topics, and I should wish to write on the same—besides, it will be less harassing to yourself to address me as usual.

'May God long preserve to you the domestic treasures you value; and when bereavement at last comes, may He give you strength to bear it.—Yours sincerely,

'C. BRONTË.'

TO W. S. WILLIAMS

'*February* 1*st*, 1849.

'My dear Sir,—Anne seems so tranquil this morning, so free from pain and fever, and looks and speaks so like herself in health, that I too feel relieved, and I take advantage of the respite to write to you, hoping that my letter may reflect something of the comparative peace I feel.

'Whether my hopes are quite fallacious or not, I do not know; but sometimes I fancy that the remedies prescribed by Mr. Teale, and approved—as I was glad to learn—by Dr. Forbes, are working a good result. Consumption, I am aware, is a flattering malady, but certainly Anne's illness has of late assumed a less alarming character than it had in the beginning: the hectic is allayed; the cough gives a more frequent reprieve. Could I but believe she would live two years—a year longer, I should be thankful: I dreaded the terrors of the swift messenger which snatched Emily from us, as it seemed, in a few days.

'The parcel came yesterday. You and Mr. Smith do nothing by halves. Neither of you care for being thanked, so I will keep my gratitude in my own mind. The choice of books is perfect. Papa is at this moment reading Macaulay's *History*, which he had wished to see. Anne is engaged with one of Frederika Bremer's tales.

'I wish I could send a parcel in return; I had hoped to have had one by this time ready to despatch. When I saw you and Mr. Smith in London, I little thought of all that was to come between July and Spring: how my thoughts were to be caught away from imagination, enlisted and absorbed in realities the most cruel.

'I will tell you what I want to do; it is to show you the first volume of my MS., which I have copied. In reading Mary Barton (a clever though painful tale) I was a little dismayed to find myself in some measure anticipated both in subject and incident. I should like to have your opinion on this point, and to know whether the resemblance appears as considerable to a stranger as it does to myself. I should wish also to have the benefit of such general strictures and advice as you choose to give. Shall I therefore send the MS. when I return the first batch of books?

'But remember, if I show it to you it is on two conditions: the first, that you give me a faithful opinion—I do not promise to be swayed by it, but I should like to have it; the second, that you show it and speak of it to *none* but Mr. Smith. I have always a great horror of premature announcements—they may do harm and can never do good. Mr. Smith must be so kind as not to mention it yet in his quarterly circulars. All human affairs are so uncertain, and my position especially is at present so peculiar, that I cannot count on the time, and would rather that no allusion should be made to a work of which great part is yet to create.

'There are two volumes in the first parcel which, having seen, I cannot bring myself to part with, and must beg Mr. Smith's permission to retain: Mr. Thackeray's *Journey from Cornhill, etc.* and *The testimony to the Truth.* That last is indeed a book after my own heart. I *do* like the mind it discloses—it is of a fine and high order. Alexander Harris may be a clown by birth, but he is a nobleman by nature. When I could read no other book, I read his and derived comfort from it. No matter whether or not I can agree in all his views, it is the principles, the feelings, the heart of the man I admire.

'Write soon and tell me whether you think it advisable that I should send the MS.—Yours sincerely,

'C. Brontë.'

TO W. S. WILLIAMS

'Haworth, *February 4th*, 1849.

'My dear Sir,—I send the parcel up without delay, according to your request. The manuscript has all its errors upon it, not having been read through since copying. I have kept *Madeline*, along with the two other books I mentioned; I shall consider it the gift of Miss Kavanagh, and shall value it both for its literary excellence and for the modest merit of the giver. We already possess Tennyson's *Poems* and *Our Street*. Emerson's *Essays* I read with much interest, and often with admiration, but they are of mixed gold and clay—deep and invigorating truth, dreary and depressing fallacy seem to me combined therein. In George Borrow's works I found a wild fascination, a vivid graphic power of description, a fresh originality, an athletic simplicity (so to speak), which give them a stamp of their own. After reading his *Bible in Spain* I felt as if I had actually travelled at his side, and seen the "wild Sil" rush from its mountain cradle; wandered in the hilly wilderness of the Sierras; encountered and conversed with Manehegan, Castillian, Andalusian, Arragonese, and, above all, with the savage Gitanos.

'Your mention of Mr. Taylor suggests to me that possibly you and Mr. Smith might wish him to share the little secret of the MS.—that exclusion might seem invidious, that it might make your mutual evening chat less pleasant. If so, admit him to the confidence by all means. He is attached to the firm, and will no doubt keep its secrets. I shall be glad of another censor, and if a severe one, so much the better, provided he is also just. I court the keenest criticism. Far rather would I never publish more, than publish anything inferior to my first effort. Be honest, therefore, all three of you. If you think this book promises less favourably than *Jane Eyre*, say so; it is but trying again, *i.e.*, if life and health be spared.

'Anne continues a little better—the mild weather suits her. At times I hear the renewal of hope's whisper, but I dare not listen too fondly; she deceived me cruelly before. A sudden change to cold would be the test. I dread such change, but must not anticipate. Spring lies before us, and then summer—surely we may hope a little!

'Anne expresses a wish to see the notices of the poems. You had better, therefore, send them. We shall expect to find painful allusions to one now above blame and beyond praise; but these must be borne. For ourselves, we are almost indifferent to censure. I read the *Quarterly* without a pang, except that I thought there were some sentences disgraceful to the critic. He seems anxious to let it be understood that he is a person well acquainted with the habits of the upper classes. Be this as it may, I am afraid he is no gentleman; and moreover, that no training could make him such.[1] Many a poor man, born and bred to labour, would disdain that reviewer's cast of feeling.—Yours sincerely,

'C. BRONTË.'

Footnotes:

[1] In his next letter Mr. Williams informed her that Miss Rigby was the writer of the Quarterly article.

TO W. S. WILLIAMS

'*March 2nd*, 1849.

'My dear Sir,—My sister still continues better: she has less languor and weakness; her spirits are improved. This change gives cause, I think, both for gratitude and hope.

'I am glad that you and Mr. Smith like the commencement of my present work. I wish it were *more than a commencement*; for how it will be reunited after the long break, or how it can gather force of flow when the current has been checked or rather drawn off so long, I know not.

'I sincerely thank you both for the candid expression of your objections. What you say with reference to the first chapter shall be duly weighed. At present I feel reluctant to withdraw it, because, as I formerly said of the Lowood part of *Jane Eyre*, *it is true*. The curates and their ongoings are merely photographed from the life. I should like you to explain to me more fully the ground of your objections. Is it because you think this chapter will render the work liable to severe handling by the press? Is it because knowing as you now do the identity of "Currer Bell," this scene strikes you as unfeminine? Is it because it is intrinsically defective and inferior? I am afraid the two first reasons would not weigh with me—the last would.

'Anne and I thought it very kind in you to preserve all the notices of the Poems so carefully for us. Some of them, as you said, were well worth reading. We were glad to find that our old friend the *Critic* has again a kind word for us. I was struck with one curious fact, viz., that four of the notices are fac-similes of each other. How does this happen? I suppose they copy.'

TO MISS ELLEN NUSSEY

'*March 8th*, 1849.

'Dear Ellen,—Anne's state has apparently varied very little during the last fortnight or three weeks. I wish I could say she gains either flesh, strength, or appetite; but there is no progress on these points, nor I hope, as far as regards the two last at least, any falling off; she is piteously thin. Her cough, and the pain in her side continue the same.

'I write these few lines that you may not think my continued silence strange; anything like frequent correspondence I cannot keep up, and you must excuse me. I trust you and all at Brookroyd are happy and well. Give my love to your mother and all the rest, and—Believe me, yours sincerely,

'C. Brontë.'

TO W. S. WILLIAMS

'*March 11th*, 1849.

'My dear Sir,—My sister has been something worse since I wrote last. We have had nearly a week of frost, and the change has tried her, as I feared it would do, though not so severely as former experience had led me to apprehend. I am thankful to say she is now again a little better. Her state of mind is usually placid, and her chief sufferings consist in the harassing cough and a sense of languor.

'I ought to have acknowledged the safe arrival of the parcel before now, but I put it off from day to day, fearing I should write a sorrowful letter. A similar apprehension induces me to abridge this note.

'Believe me, whether in happiness or the contrary, yours sincerely,

'C. Brontë.'

TO MISS LÆTITIA WHEELWRIGHT

'Haworth, *March* 15*th*, 1849.

'Dear Lætitia,—I have not quite forgotten you through the winter, but I have remembered you only like some pleasant waking idea struggling through a dreadful dream. You say my last letter was dated September 14th. You ask how I have passed the time since. What has happened to me? Why have I been silent?

'It is soon told.

'On the 24th of September my only brother, after being long in weak health, and latterly consumptive—though we were far from apprehending immediate danger—died, quite suddenly as it seemed to us. He had been out two days before. The shock was great. Ere he could be interred I fell ill. A low nervous fever left me very weak. As I was slowly recovering, my sister Emily, whom you knew, was seized with inflammation of the lungs; suppuration took place; two agonising months of hopes and fears followed, and on the 19th of December *she died*.

'She was scarcely cold in her grave when Anne, my youngest and last sister, who has been delicate all her life, exhibited symptoms that struck us with acute alarm. We sent for the first advice that could be procured. She was examined with the stethoscope, and the dreadful fact was announced that her lungs too were affected, and that tubercular consumption had already made considerable progress. A system of treatment was prescribed, which has since been ratified by the opinion of Dr. Forbes, whom your papa will, I dare say, know. I hope it has somewhat delayed disease. She is now a patient invalid, and I am her nurse. God has hitherto supported me in some sort through all these bitter calamities, and my father, I am thankful to say, has been wonderfully sustained; but there have been hours, days, weeks of inexpressible anguish to undergo, and the cloud of impending distress still lowers dark and sullen above us. I cannot write much. I can only pray Providence to preserve you and yours from such affliction as He has seen good to accumulate on me and mine.

'With best regards to your dear mamma and all your circle,— Believe me, yours faithfully,

'C. Brontë.'

TO MISS WOOLER

'Haworth, *March* 24*th*, 1849.

'My dear Miss Wooler,—I have delayed answering your letter in the faint hope that I might be able to reply favourably to your inquiries after my sister's health. This, however, is not permitted me to do. Her decline is gradual and fluctuating, but its nature is not doubtful. The symptoms of cough, pain in the side and chest, wasting of flesh, strength, and appetite, after the sad experience we have had, cannot but be regarded by us as equivocal.

'In spirit she is resigned; at heart she is, I believe, a true Christian. She looks beyond this life, and regards her home and rest as elsewhere than on earth. May God support her and all of us through the trial of lingering sickness, and aid her in the last hour when the struggle which separates soul from body must be gone through!

'We saw Emily torn from the midst of us when our hearts clung to her with intense attachment, and when, loving each other as we did—well, it seemed as if (might we but have been spared to each other) we could have found complete happiness in our mutual society and affection. She was scarcely buried when Anne's health failed, and we were warned that consumption had found another victim in her, and that it would be vain to reckon on her life.

'These things would be too much if Reason, unsupported by Religion, were condemned to bear them alone. I have cause to be most thankful for the strength which has hitherto been vouchsafed both to my father and myself. God, I think, is specially merciful to old age; and for my own part, trials which in prospective would have seemed to me quite intolerable, when they actually came, I endured without prostration. Yet, I must confess, that in the time which has elapsed since Emily's death, there have been moments of solitary, deep, inert affliction, far harder to bear than those which immediately followed our loss. The crisis of bereavement has an acute pang which goads to exertion, the desolate after-feeling sometimes paralyses.

'I have learned that we are not to find solace in our own strength: we must seek it in God's omnipotence. Fortitude is good, but fortitude itself must be shaken under us to teach us how weak we are.

'With best wishes to yourself and all dear to you, and sincere thanks for the interest you so kindly continue to take in me and my sister,—Believe me, my dear Miss Wooler, yours faithfully,

'C. BRONTË.'

TO W. S. WILLIAMS

'*April* 16*th*, 1849.

'My dear Sir,—Your kind advice on the subject of Homœopathy deserves and has our best thanks. We find ourselves, however, urged from more than one quarter to try different systems and medicines, and I fear we have already given offence by not listening to all. The fact is, were we in every instance compliant, my dear sister would be harassed by continual changes. Cod-liver oil and carbonate of iron were first strongly recommended. Anne took them as long as she could, but at last she was obliged to give them up: the oil yielded her no nutriment, it did not arrest the progress of emaciation, and as it kept her always sick, she was prevented from taking food of any sort. Hydropathy was then strongly advised. She is now trying Gobold's Vegetable Balsam; she thinks it does her some good; and as it is the first medicine which has had that effect, she would wish to persevere with it for a time. She is also looking hopefully forward to deriving benefit from change of air. We have obtained Mr. Teale's permission to go to the seaside in the course of six or eight weeks. At first I felt torn between two duties—that of staying with papa and going with Anne; but as it is papa's own most kindly expressed wish that I should adopt the latter plan, and as, besides, he is now, thank God! in tolerable health, I hope to be spared the pain of resigning the care of my sister to other hands, however friendly. We wish to keep together as long as we can. I hope, too, to derive from the change some renewal of physical strength and mental composure (in neither of which points am I what I ought or wish to be) to make me a better and more cheery nurse.

'I fear I must have seemed to you hard in my observations about *The Emigrant Family*. The fact was, I compared Alexander Harris with himself only. It is not equal to the *Testimony to the Truth*, but, tried by the standard of other and very popular books too, it is very clever and original. Both subject and the manner of treating it are unhackneyed: he gives new views of new scenes and furnishes interesting information on interesting topics. Considering the increasing necessity for and tendency to emigration, I should think it has a fair chance of securing the success it merits.

'I took up Leigh Hunt's book *The Town* with the impression that it would be interesting only to Londoners, and I was surprised, ere I had read many pages, to find myself enchained by his pleasant, graceful, easy style, varied knowledge, just views, and kindly spirit. There is something peculiarly anti-melancholic in Leigh Hunt's writings, and yet they are never boisterous. They resemble sunshine, being at once bright and tranquil.

'I like Carlyle better and better. His style I do not like, nor do I always concur in his opinions, nor quite fall in with his hero worship; but there is a manly love of truth, an honest recognition and fearless vindication of intrinsic greatness, of intellectual and moral worth, considered apart from birth, rank, or wealth, which commands my sincere admiration. Carlyle would never do for a contributor to the *Quarterly*. I have not read his *French Revolution*.

'I congratulate you on the approaching publication of Mr. Ruskin's new work. If the *Seven Lamps of Architecture* resemble their predecessor, *Modern Painters*, they will be no lamps at all, but a new constellation—seven bright stars, for whose rising the reading world ought to be anxiously agaze.

'Do not ask me to mention what books I should like to read. Half the pleasure of receiving a parcel from Cornhill consists in having its contents chosen for us. We like to discover, too, by the leaves cut here and there, that the ground has been travelled before us. I may however say, with reference to works of fiction, that I should much like to see one of Godwin's works, never having hitherto had that pleasure—*Caleb Williams* or *Fleetwood*, or which you thought best worth reading.

'But it is yet much too soon to talk of sending more books;

our present stock is scarcely half exhausted. You will perhaps think I am a slow reader, but remember, Currer Bell is a country housewife, and has sundry little matters connected with the needle and kitchen to attend to which take up half his day, especially now when, alas! there is but one pair of hands where once there were three. I did not mean to touch that chord, its sound is too sad.

'I try to write now and then. The effort was a hard one at first. It renewed the terrible loss of last December strangely. Worse than useless did it seem to attempt to write what there no longer lived an "Ellis Bell" to read; the whole book, with every hope founded on it, faded to vanity and vexation of spirit.

'One inducement to persevere and do my best I still have, however, and I am thankful for it: I should like to please my kind friends at Cornhill. To that end I wish my powers would come back; and if it would please Providence to restore my remaining sister, I think they would.

'Do not forget to tell me how you are when you write again. I trust your indisposition is quite gone by this time.—Believe me, yours sincerely,

'C. BRONTË.'

TO MISS ELLEN NUSSEY

'*May* 1*st*, 1849.

'Dear Ellen,—I returned Mary Taylor's letter to Hunsworth as soon as I had read it. Thank God she was safe up to that time, but I do not think the earthquake was then over. I shall long to hear tidings of her again.

'Anne was worse during the warm weather we had about a

week ago. She grew weaker, and both the pain in her side and her cough were worse; strange to say, since it is colder, she has appeared rather to revive than sink. I still hope that if she gets over May she may last a long time.

'We have engaged lodgings at Scarbro'. We stipulated for a good-sized sitting-room and an airy double-bedded lodging room, with a sea view, and if not deceived, have obtained these desiderata at No. 2 Cliff. Anne says it is one of the best situations in the place. It would not have done to have taken lodgings either in the town or on the bleak steep coast, where Miss Wooler's house is situated. If Anne is to get any good she must have every advantage. Miss Outhwaite [her godmother] left her in her will a legacy of £200, and she cannot employ her money better than in obtaining what may prolong existence, if it does not restore health. We hope to leave home on the 23rd, and I think it will be advisable to rest at York, and stay all night there. I hope this arrangement will suit you. We reckon on your society, dear Ellen, as a real privilege and pleasure. We shall take little luggage, and shall have to buy bonnets and dresses and several other things either at York or Scarbro'; which place do you think would be best? Oh, if it would please God to strengthen and revive Anne, how happy we might be together! His will, however, must be done, and if she is not to recover, it remains to pray for strength and patience.

'C. B.'

TO W. S. WILLIAMS

'*May 8th*, 1849.

'My dear Sir,—I hasten to acknowledge the two kind letters for which I am indebted to you. That fine spring weather of which you speak did not bring such happiness to us in its sunshine as I trust it did to you and thousands besides—the change proved trying to my sister. For a week or ten days I did not know what to think, she became so weak, and suffered so much from increased pain in the side, and aggravated cough. The last few days have been much colder, yet, strange to say, during their continuance she has appeared rather to revive than sink. She not unfrequently shows the very same symptoms which were apparent in Emily only a few days before she died—fever in the evenings, sleepless nights, and a sort of lethargy in the morning hours; this creates acute anxiety—then comes an improvement, which reassures. In about three weeks, should the weather be genial and her strength continue at all equal to the journey, we hope to go to Scarboro'. It is not without misgiving that I contemplate a departure from home under such circumstances; but since she herself earnestly wishes the experiment to be tried, I think it ought not to be neglected. We are in God's hands, and must trust the results to Him. An old school-fellow of mine, a tried and faithful friend, has volunteered to accompany us. I shall have the satisfaction of leaving papa to the attentions of two servants equally tried and faithful. One of them is indeed now old and infirm, and unfit to stir much from her chair by the kitchen fireside; but the other is young and active, and even she has lived with us seven years. I have reason, therefore, you see, to be thankful amidst sorrow, especially as papa still possesses every faculty unimpaired, and though not robust, has good general health—a sort of chronic cough is his sole complaint.

'I hope Mr. Smith will not risk a cheap edition of *Jane Eyre* yet, he had better wait awhile—the public will be sick of the name of that one book. I can make no promise as to when another will be ready—neither my time nor my efforts are my own. That absorption in my employment to which I gave myself up without fear of doing wrong when I wrote *Jane Eyre*, would now be alike impossible and blamable; but I do what I can, and have made some little progress. We must all be patient.

'Meantime, I should say, let the public forget at their ease, and let us not be nervous about it. And as to the critics, if the Bells possess real merit, I do not fear impartial justice being rendered them one day. I have a very short mental as well as physical sight in some matters, and am far less uneasy at the idea of public impatience, misconstruction, censure, etc., than I am at the thought of the anxiety of those two or three friends in Cornhill to whom I owe much kindness, and whose expectations I would earnestly wish not to disappoint. If they can make up their minds to wait tranquilly, and put some confidence in my goodwill, if not my power, to get on as well as may be, I shall not repine; but I verily believe that the "nobler sex" find it more difficult to wait, to plod, to work out their destiny inch by inch, than their sisters do. They are always for walking so fast and taking such long steps, one cannot keep up with them. One should never tell a gentleman that one has commenced a task till it is nearly achieved. Currer Bell, even if he had no let or hindrance, and if his path were quite smooth, could never march with the tread of a Scott, a Bulwer, a Thackeray, or a Dickens. I want you and Mr. Smith clearly to understand this. I have always wished to guard you against exaggerated anticipations—calculate low when you calculate on me. An honest man—and woman too—would always rather rise above expectation than fall below it.

'Have I lectured enough? and am I understood?

'Give my sympathising respects to Mrs. Williams. I hope her little daughter is by this time restored to perfect health. It pleased me to see with what satisfaction you speak of your son. I was glad, too, to hear of the progress and welfare of Miss Kavanagh.

The notices of Mr. Harris's works are encouraging and just—may they contribute to his success!

'Should Mr. Thackeray again ask after Currer Bell, say the secret is and will be well kept because it is not worth disclosure. This fact his own sagacity will have already led him to divine. In the hope that it may not be long ere I hear from you again,— Believe me, yours sincerely,

'C. BRONTË.'

TO MISS WOOLER

'Haworth, *May* 16*th*, 1849.

'My dear Miss Wooler,—I will lose no time in thanking you for your letter and kind offer of assistance. We have, however, already engaged lodgings. I am not myself acquainted with Scarbro', but Anne knows it well, having been there three or four times. She had a particular preference for the situation of some lodgings (No. 2 Cliff). We wrote about them, and finding them disengaged, took them. Your information is, notwithstanding, valuable, should we find this place in any way ineligible. It is a satisfaction to be provided with directions for future use.

'Next Wednesday is the day fixed for our departure. Ellen Nussey accompanies us (by Anne's expressed wish). I could not refuse her society, but I dared not urge her to go, for I have little hope that the excursion will be one of pleasure or benefit to those engaged in it. Anne is extremely weak. She herself has a fixed impression that the sea air will give her a chance of regaining strength; that chance, therefore, we must have. Having resolved to try the experiment, misgivings are useless; and yet, when I look at her, misgivings will rise. She is more emaciated than Emily was at the very last; her breath scarcely serves her to mount the stairs, however slowly. She sleeps very little at night, and often passes most of the forenoon in a semi-lethargic state. Still, she is up all day, and even goes out a little when it is fine. Fresh air usually acts as a stimulus, but its reviving power diminishes.

'With best wishes for your own health and welfare,—Believe me, my dear Miss Wooler, yours sincerely,

'C. BRONTË.'

TO W. S. WILLIAMS

'No. 2 Cliff, Scarboro', *May 27th*, 1849.

'My dear Sir,—The date above will inform you why I have not answered your last letter more promptly. I have been busy with preparations for departure and with the journey. I am thankful to say we reached our destination safely, having rested one night at York. We found assistance wherever we needed it; there was always an arm ready to do for my sister what I was not quite strong enough to do: lift her in and out of the carriages, carry her across the line, etc.

'It made her happy to see both York and its Minster, and Scarboro' and its bay once more. There is yet no revival of bodily strength—I fear indeed the slow ebb continues. People who see her tell me I must not expect her to last long—but it is something to cheer her mind.

'Our lodgings are pleasant. As Anne sits at the window she can look down on the sea, which this morning is calm as glass. She says if she could breathe more freely she would be comfortable at this moment—but she cannot breathe freely.

'My friend Ellen is with us. I find her presence a solace. She is a calm, steady girl—not brilliant, but good and true. She suits and has always suited me well. I like her, with her phlegm, repose, sense, and sincerity, better than I should like the most talented without these qualifications.

'If ever I see you again I should have pleasure in talking over with you the topics you allude to in your last—or rather, in hearing *you* talk them over. We see these things through a glass darkly—or at least I see them thus. So far from objecting to speculation on, or discussion of, the subject, I should wish to hear what others have to say. By *others*, I mean only the serious and reflective—levity in such matters shocks as much as hypocrisy.

'Write to me. In this strange place your letters will come like the visits of a friend. Fearing to lose the post, I will add no more at present.—Believe me, yours sincerely,

'C. BRONTË.'

TO W. S. WILLIAMS

'*May* 30*th*, 1849.

'My dear Sir,—My poor sister is taken quietly home at last. She died on Monday. With almost her last breath she said she was happy, and thanked God that death was come, and come so gently. I did not think it would be so soon.

'You will not expect me to add more at present.—Yours faithfully,

'C. BRONTË.'

TO W. S. WILLIAMS

'*June 25th*, 1849.

'My dear Sir,—I am now again at home, where I returned last Thursday. I call it *home* still—much as London would be called London if an earthquake should shake its streets to ruins. But let me not be ungrateful: Haworth parsonage is still a home for me, and not quite a ruined or desolate home either. Papa is there, and two most affectionate and faithful servants, and two old dogs, in their way as faithful and affectionate—Emily's large house-dog which lay at the side of her dying bed, and followed her funeral to the vault, lying in the pew couched at our feet while the burial service was being read—and Anne's little spaniel. The ecstasy of these poor animals when I came in was something singular. At former returns from brief absences they always welcomed me warmly—but not in that strange, heart-touching way. I am certain they thought that, as I was returned, my sisters were not far behind. But here my sisters will come no more. Keeper may visit Emily's little bed-room—as he still does day by day—and Flossy may look wistfully round for Anne, they will never see them again—nor shall I—at least the human part of me. I must not write so sadly, but how can I help thinking and feeling sadly? In the daytime effort and occupation aid me, but when evening darkens, something in my heart revolts against the burden of solitude—the sense of loss and want grows almost too much for me. I am not good or amiable in such moments, I am rebellious, and it is only the thought of my dear father in the next room, or of the kind servants in the kitchen, or some caress from the poor dogs, which restores me to softer sentiments and more rational views. As to the night—could I do without bed, I would never seek it. Waking, I think, sleeping, I dream of them; and I cannot recall them as they were in health, still they appear to me in sickness and suffering. Still, my nights were worse after the first shock of Branwell's death—they were terrible then; and the impressions experienced on waking were at that time such as we do not put into language. Worse seemed at hand than was yet endured—in truth, worse awaited us.

'All this bitterness must be tasted. Perhaps the palate will grow used to the draught in time, and find its flavour less acrid. This pain must be undergone; its poignancy, I trust, will be blunted one day. Ellen would have come back with me but I would not let her. I knew it would be better to face the desolation at once—later or sooner the sharp pang must be experienced.

'Labour must be the cure, not sympathy. Labour is the only radical cure for rooted sorrow. The society of a calm, serenely cheerful companion—such as Ellen—soothes pain like a soft opiate, but I find it does not probe or heal the wound; sharper, more severe means, are necessary to make a remedy. Total change might do much; where that cannot be obtained, work is the best substitute.

'I by no means ask Miss Kavanagh to write to me. Why should she trouble herself to do it? What claim have I on her? She does not know me—she cannot care for me except vaguely and on hearsay. I have got used to your friendly sympathy, and it comforts me. I have tried and trust the fidelity of one or two other friends, and I lean upon it. The natural affection of my father and the attachment and solicitude of our two servants are precious and consolatory to me, but I do not look round for general pity; conventional condolence I do not want, either from man or woman.

'The letter you inclosed in your last bore the signature H. S. Mayers—the address, Sheepscombe, Stroud, Gloucestershire; can you give me any information respecting the writer? It is my intention to acknowledge it one day. I am truly glad to hear that your little invalid is restored to health, and that the rest of your family continue well. Mrs. Williams should spare herself for her husband's and children's sake. Her life and health are too valuable to those round her to be lavished—she should be careful of them.—Believe me, yours sincerely,

'C. BRONTË.'

It is not necessary to tell over again the story of Anne's death. Miss Ellen Nussey, who was an eye witness, has related it once for all in Mrs. Gaskell's Memoir. The tomb at Scarborough hears the following inscription:—

Here Lie the Remains of
ANNE BRONTË
DAUGHTER OF THE REV. P. BRONTË
Incumbent of Haworth, Yorkshire
She Died, Aged 28, May 28th, 1849

AN EXCERPT FROM
Charlotte Bronte and Her Circle, 1896

THE SISTERS BRONTË

BY MRS OLIPHANT

The effect produced upon the general mind by the appearance of Charlotte Brontë in literature, and afterwards by the record of her life when that was over, is one which it is nowadays somewhat difficult to understand. Had the age been deficient in the art of fiction, or had it followed any long level of mediocrity in that art, we could have comprehended this more easily. But Charlotte Brontë appeared in the full flush of a period more richly endowed than any other we know of in that special branch of literature, so richly endowed, indeed, that the novel had taken quite fictitious importance, and the names of Dickens and Thackeray ranked almost higher than those of any living writers except perhaps Tennyson, then young and on his promotion too. Anthony Trollope and Charles Reade who, though in their day extremely popular, have never had justice from a public which now seems almost to have forgotten them, formed a powerful second rank to these two great names. It is a great addition to the value of the distinction gained by the new comer that it was acquired in an age so rich in the qualities of the imagination.

But this only increases the wonder of a triumph which had no artificial means to heighten it, nothing but genius on the part of a writer possessing little experience or knowledge of the world, and no sort of social training or adventitious aid. The genius was indeed unmistakable, and possessed in a very high degree the power of expressing itself in the most vivid and actual pictures of life. But the life of which it had command was seldom attractive, often narrow, local, and of a kind which meant keen personal satire more than any broader view of human existence. A group of commonplace clergymen, intense against their little parochial background as only the most real art of portraiture, intensified by individual scorn and dislike, could have made them: the circle of limited interests, small emulations, keen little spites and rancours, filling the atmosphere of a great boarding school, the Brussels *Pensionnat des filles*—these were the two spheres chiefly portrayed: but portrayed with an absolute untempered force which knew neither charity, softness, nor even impartiality, but burned upon the paper and made everything round dim in the contrast. I imagine it was this extraordinary naked force which was the great cause of a success, never perhaps like the numerical successes in literature of the present day, when edition follows edition, and thousand thousand, of the books which are the favourites of the public: but one which has lived and lasted through nearly half a century, and is even now potent enough to carry on a little literature of its own, book after book following each other not so much to justify as to reproclaim and echo to all the winds the fame originally won. No one else of the century, I think, has called forth this persevering and lasting homage. Not Dickens, though perhaps more of him than of any one else has been dealt out at intervals to an admiring public; not Thackeray, of whom still we know but little; not George Eliot, though her fame has more solid foundations than that of Miss Brontë. Scarcely Scott has called forth more continual droppings of elucidation, explanation, remark. Yet the books upon which this tremendous reputation is founded though vivid, original, and striking in the highest degree, are not great books. Their philosophy of life is that of a schoolgirl, their knowledge of the world almost *nil*, their conclusions confused by the haste and passion of a mind self-centred and working in the narrowest orbit. It is rather, as we have said, the most incisive and realistic art of portraiture than any exercise of the nobler arts of fiction—imagination, combination, construction—or humorous survey of life or deep apprehension of its problems—upon which this fame is built.

The curious circumstance that Charlotte Brontë was, if the word may be so used, doubled by her sisters, the elder, Emily, whose genius has been taken for granted, carrying the wilder elements of the common inspiration to extremity in the strange, chaotic and weird romance of "Wuthering Heights," while Anne diluted such powers of social observation as were in the family into two mildly disagreeable novels of a much commoner order, has no doubt also enhanced the central figure of the group to an amazing degree. They placed her strength in relief by displaying its separate elements, and thus commending the higher skill and larger spirit which took in both, understanding the moors and wild country and rude image of man better than the one, and misunderstanding the common course of more subdued life less than the other. The three together are for ever inseparable; they were homely, lowly, somewhat neglected in their lives, had few opportunities and few charms to the careless eye: yet no group of women, undistinguished by rank, unendowed by beauty, and known to but a limited circle of friends as unimportant as themselves have ever, I think, in the course of history—certainly never in this century—come to such universal recognition. The effect is quite unique, unprecedented, and difficult to account for; but there cannot be the least doubt that it is a matter of absolute fact which nobody can deny.

* * * * *

These three daughters of a poor country clergyman came into the world early in the century, the dates of their births being 1816, 1818, 1820, in the barest of little parsonages in the midst of the moors—a wild but beautiful country, and a rough but highly characteristic and keen-witted people. Yorkshire is the very heart of England; its native force, its keen practical sense, its rough wit, and the unfailing importance in the nation of the largest of the shires has given it a strong individual character and position almost like that of an independent province. But the Brontës, whose name is a softened and decorated edition of a common Irish name, were not of that forcible race: and perhaps the strong strain after emotion, and revolt against the monotonies of life, which were so conspicuous in them were more easily traceable to their Celtic origin than many other developments attributed to that cause. They were motherless from an early age, children of a father who, after having been depicted as a capricious tyrant, seems now to have found a fairer representation as a man with a high spirit and peculiar temper, yet neither unkind to his family nor uninterested in their welfare. There was one son, once supposed to be the hero and victim of a disagreeable romance, but apparent now as only a specimen, not alas, uncommon, of the ordinary ne'er-do-well of a family, without force of character or self-control to keep his place with decency in the world.

These children all scribbled from their infancy as soon as the power of inscribing words upon paper was acquired by them, inventing imaginary countries and compiling visionary records of them as so many imaginative children do. The elder girl and boy made one pair, the younger girls another, connected by the closest links of companionship. It was thought or hoped that the son was the genius of the family, and at the earliest possible age he began to send his effusions to editors, and to seek admission to magazines with the mingled arrogance and humility of a half-fledged creature. But the world knows now that it was not poor Branwell who was the genius of the family; and this injury done him in his cradle, and the evil report of him that everybody gives throughout his life, awakens a certain pity in the mind for the unfortunate youth so unable to keep any supremacy among the girls whom he must have considered his natural inferiors and vassals. We are told by Charlotte Brontë herself that he never knew of the successes of his sisters, the fact of their successive publications being concealed from him out of tenderness for his feelings; but it is scarcely to be credited that when the parish knew the unfortunate brother did not find out. The unhappy attempt of Mrs. Gaskell in writing the lives of the sisters to make this melancholy young man accountable for the almost brutal element in Emily Brontë's conception of life, and the strange views of Charlotte as to what men were capable of, has made him far too important in their history; where, indeed, he had no need to have appeared at all, had the family pride consisted, as the pride of so many families does, in veiling rather than exhibiting the faults of its members. So far as can be made out now, he had as little as possible to do with their development in any way.

There was nothing unnatural or out of the common in the youthful life of the family except that strange gift of genius, which though consistent with every genial quality of being, in such a nature as that of Scott, seems in other developments of character to turn all the elements into chaos. Its effect upon the parson's three daughters was, indeed, not of a very wholesome kind. It awakened in them an uneasy sense of superiority which gave double force to every one of the little hardships which a girl in a great school of a charitable kind, and a governess in a middle-class house, has to support: and made life harder instead of sweeter to them in many ways, since it was full of the biting experience of conditions less favourable than those of many persons round them whom they could not but feel inferior to themselves.

The great school, which it was Charlotte Brontë's first act when she began her literary career to invest with an almost tragic character of misery, privation, and wrong, was her first step from home. Yorkshire schools did not at that period enjoy a very good reputation in the world, and Nicholas Nickleby was forming his acquaintance with the squalid cruelty of Dotheboys Hall just about the same time when Charlotte Brontë's mind was being filled with the privations and discontents of Lowood. In such a case there is generally some fire where there is so much smoke, and probably Lowood was under no very heavenly *régime*: but at the same time its drawbacks were sharply accentuated by that keen criticism which is suggested by the constant sense of injured worth and consciousness of a superiority not acknowledged. The same feeling pursued her into the situations as governess which she occupied one after another, and in which her indignation at being expected to feel affection for the children put under her charge, forms a curious addition to the other grievances with which fate pursues her life. No doubt there are many temptations in the life of a governess; the position of a silent observer in a household, looking on at all its mistakes, and seeing the imperfection of its management with double force because of the effect they have on herself—especially if she feels herself competent, had she but the power, to set things right— must always be a difficult one. It was not continued long enough, however, to involve very much suffering; though no doubt it helped to mature the habit of sharp personal criticism and war with the world.

At the same time Charlotte Brontë made some very warm personal friendships, and wrote a great many letters to the school friends who pleased her, in which a somewhat stilted tone and demure seriousness is occasionally invaded by the usual chatter of girlhood, to the great improvement of the atmosphere if not of the mind. Ellen Nussey, Mary Taylor, women not manifestly intellectual but sensible and independent without either exaggeration of sentiment or hint of tragic story, remained her close friends as long as she lived, and her letters to them, though always a little demure, give us a gentler idea of her than anything else she has written. Not that there is much charm either of style or subject in them: but there is no sort of bitterness or sense of insufficient appreciation. Nothing can be more usual and commonplace, indeed, than this portion of her life. As in so many cases, the artificial lights thrown upon it by theories formed afterwards, clear away when we examine its actual records, and it is apparent that there was neither exceptional harshness of circumstance nor internal struggle in the existence of the girl who, though more or less in arms against everybody outside—especially when holding a position superior to her own, more especially still when exercising authority over her in any way—was yet quite an easy-minded, not unhappy, young woman at home, with friends to whom she could pour out long pages of what is, on the whole, quite moderate and temperate criticism of life, not without cheerful allusion to now and then a chance curate or other young person of the opposite sex, suspected of "paying attention" to one or other of the little coterie. These allusions are not more lofty or dignified than are similar notes of girls of less exalted pretensions, but there is not a touch in them of the keen pointed pen which afterwards put up the Haworth curates in all their imperfections before the world.

The other sisters at this time in the background, two figures always clinging together, looking almost like one, have no great share in this softer part of Charlotte's life. They were, though so different in character, completely devoted to each other, apparently forming no other friendships, each content with the one other partaker of her every thought. A little literature seems to have been created between them, little chapters of recollection and commentary upon their life, sealed up and put away for three years in each case, to be opened on Emily's or on Anne's birthday alternately, as a pathetic sign of their close unity, though the little papers were in themselves simple in the extreme. Anne too became a governess with something of the same experience as Charlotte, and uttering very hard judgments of unconscious people who were not the least unkind to her. But Emily had no such trials. She remained at home perhaps because she was too uncompromising to be allowed to make the experiment of putting up with other people, perhaps because one daughter at home was indispensable. The family seems to have had kind and trusted old servants, so that the cares of housekeeping did not weigh heavily upon the daughter in charge, and there is no evidence of exceptional hardness or roughness in their circumstances in any way.

In 1842, Charlotte and Emily, aged respectively twenty-six and twenty-four, went to Brussels. Their design was "to acquire a thorough familiarity with French," also some insight into other languages, with the view of setting up a school on their own account. The means were supplied by the aunt, who had lived in their house and taken more or less care of them since their mother's death. The two sisters were nearly a year in the Pensionnat Héger, now so perfectly known in every detail of its existence to all who have read "Villette." They were recalled by the death of the kind aunt who had procured them this advantage, and afterwards Charlotte, no one quite knows why, went back to Brussels for a second year, in which all her impressions were probably strengthened and intensified. Certainly a more clear and lifelike picture, scathing in its cold yet fierce light, was never made than that of the white tall Brussels house, its class rooms, its gardens, its hum of unamiable girls, its sharp display of rancorous and shrill teachers, its one inimitable professor. It startles the reader to find—a fact which we had forgotten—that M. Paul Emmanuel was M. Héger, the husband of Madame Héger and legitimate head of the house: and that this daring and extraordinary girl did not hesitate to encounter gossip or slander by making him so completely the hero of her romance. Slander in its commonplace form had nothing to do with such a fiery spirit as that of Charlotte Brontë: but it shows her perfect independence of mind and scorn of comment that she should have done this. In the end of '43 she returned home, and the episode was over. It was really the only episode of possible practical significance in her life until we come to the records of her brief literary career and her marriage, both towards its end.

* * * * *

The prospect of the school which the three sisters were to set up together was abandoned; there was no more talk of governessing. We are not told if it was the small inheritance of the aunt—only, Mr. Clement Shorter informs us, £1500—which enabled the sisters henceforward to remain at home without thought of further effort: but certainly this was what happened. And the lives of the two younger were drawing so near the end that it is a comfort to think that they enjoyed this moment of comparative grace together. Their life was extremely silent, secluded, and apart. There was the melancholy figure of Branwell to distract the house with the spectacle of heavy idleness, drink, and disorder; but this can scarcely have been so great an affliction as if he had been a more beloved brother. He was not, however, veiled by any tender attempt to cover his follies or wickedness, but openly complained of to all their friends, which mitigates the affliction: and they seem to have kept very separate from him, living in a world of their own.

In 1846 a volume of poems by Currer, Ellis, and Acton Bell, was published at their own cost. It had not the faintest success; they were informed by the publisher that two copies only had been sold, and the only satisfaction that remained to them was to send a few copies to some of the owners of those great names which the enthusiastic young women had worshipped from afar as stars in the firmament. These poems were re-published after Charlotte Brontë had attained her first triumph, and people had begun to cry out and wonder over "Wuthering Heights." The history of "Jane Eyre," on the other hand, is that of most works which have been the beginning of a career. It fell into the hands of the right man, the "reader" of Messrs. Smith, Elder and Co., Mr. Williams, a man of great intelligence and literary insight. The first story written by Charlotte Brontë, which was called "The Professor," and was the original of "Villette," written at a time when her mind was very full of the emotions raised by that singular portion of her life, had been rejected by a number of publishers, and was also rejected by Mr. Williams, who found it at once too crude and too *short* for the risks of publication, three volumes at that period being your only possible form for fiction. But he saw the power in it, and begged the author to try again at greater length. She did so; not on the basis of the "Professor" as might have seemed natural—probably the materials were still too much at fever-heat in her mind to be returned to at that moment—but by the story of "Jane Eyre," which at once placed Charlotte Brontë amid the most popular and powerful writers of her time.

I remember well the extraordinary thrill of interest which in the midst of all the Mrs. Gores, Mrs. Marshs, &c.—the latter name is mentioned along with those of Thackeray and Dickens even by Mr. Williams—came upon the reader who, in the calm of ignorance, took up the first volume of "Jane Eyre." The period of the heroine in white muslin, the immaculate creature who was of sweetness and goodness all compact, had lasted in the common lines of fiction up to that time. Miss Austen indeed might well have put an end to that abstract and empty fiction, yet it continued, as it always does continue more or less, the primitive ideal. But "Jane Eyre" gave her, for the moment, the *coup de grace*. That the book should be the story of a governess was perhaps necessary to the circumstances of the writer: and the governess was already a favourite figure in fiction. But generally she was of the beautiful, universally fascinating, all-enduring kind, the amiable blameless creature whose secret merits were never so hidden but that they might be perceived by a keen sighted hero. I am not sure, indeed, that anybody believed Miss Brontë when she said her heroine was plain. It is very clear from the story that Jane was never unnoticed, never failed to please, except among the women, whom it is the instinctive art of the novelist to rouse in arms against the central figure, thus demonstrating the jealousy, spite, and rancour native to their minds in respect to the women who please men. No male cynic was ever stronger on that subject than this typical woman. She cannot have believed it, I presume, since her closest friends were women, and she seems to have had perfect faith in their kindness: but this is a matter of conventional belief which has nothing to do with individual experience. It is one of the doctrines unassailable of the art of fiction; a thirty-ninth article in which every writer of novels is bound to believe.

Miss Brontë did not know fine ladies, and therefore, in spite of herself and a mind the reverse of vulgar, she made the competitors for Mr. Rochester's favour rather brutal and essentially vulgar persons, an error, curiously enough, which seems to have been followed by George Eliot in the corresponding scenes in "Mr. Gilfil's Love Story," where Captain Wybrow's *fiancée* treats poor Tiny very much as the beauty in Mr. Rochester's house treats Jane Eyre. Both were imaginary pictures, which perhaps more or less excuses their untruthfulness in writers both so sincere and lifelike in treating things they knew. It is amusing to remember that Jane Eyre's ignorance of dress gave a clinching argument to Miss Rigby in the *Quarterly* to decide that the writer was not and could not possibly be a woman. The much larger and more significant fact that no man (until in quite recent days when there have been instances of such effeminate art) ever made a woman so entirely the subject and inspiration of his book, the only interest in it, was entirely overlooked in what was, notwithstanding, the very shrewd and telling argument about the dress.

The chief thing, however, that distressed the candid and as yet unaccustomed reader in "Jane Eyre," and made him hope that it might be a man who had written it, was the character of Rochester's confidences to the girl whom he loved—not the character of Rochester, which was completely a woman's view, but that he should have talked to a girl so evidently innocent of his amours and his mistresses. This, however, I think, though, as we should have thought, a subject so abhorrent to a young woman such as Charlotte Brontë was, was also emphatically a woman's view. A man might have credited another man of Rochester's kind with impulses practically more heinous and designs of the worst kind: but he would not have made him err in that way.

In this was a point of honour which the woman did not understand. It marks a curious and subtle difference between the sexes. The woman less enlightened in practical evil considers less the risks of actual vice; but her imagination is free in other ways, and she innocently permits her hero to do and say things so completely against the code which is binding on gentlemen whether vicious or otherwise that her want of perception becomes conspicuous. The fact that the writer of the review in the *Quarterly* was herself a woman accounts for her mistake in supposing that the book was written if not by a man, by "a woman unsexed;" "a woman who had forfeited the society of her sex." And afterwards, when Mrs. Gaskell made her disastrous statements about Branwell Brontë and other associates of Charlotte's youth, it was with the hope of proving that the speech and manners of the men to whom she had been accustomed were of a nature to justify her in any such misapprehension of the usual manners of gentlemen. It was on the contrary, as I think, only the bold and unfettered imagination of a woman quite ignorant on all such subjects which could have suggested this special error. The mind of such a woman, casting about for something to make her wicked but delightful hero do by way of demonstrating his wickedness, yet preserving the fascination which she meant him to retain, probably hit upon this as the very wickedest thing she could think of, yet still attractive: for is there not a thrill of curiosity in searching out what such a strange being might think or say, which is of itself a strong sensation? Miss Brontë was, I think, the first to give utterance to that curiosity of the woman in respect to the man, and fascination of interest in him—not the ideal man, not Sir Kenneth, too reverent for anything but silent worship—which has since risen to such heights of speculation, and imprints now a tone upon modern fiction at which probably she would have been horrified.

* * * * *

There were numberless stories in those days of guilty love and betrayal, of how "lovely woman stoops to folly," and all the varieties of that endless subject; but it was, except in the comic vein, or with grotesque treatment, the pursuit of the woman by the man, the desire of the lover for the beloved which was the aim of fiction. A true lady of romance walked superior: she accepted (or not) the devotion: she stooped from her white height to reward her adorer: but that she herself should condescend to seek him (except under the circumstances of fashionable life, where everybody is in quest of a coronet), or call out for him to heaven and earth when he tarried in his coming, was unknown to the situations of romantic art. When the second of Charlotte Brontë's books appeared, there was accordingly quite a new sensation in store for the public. The young women in "Shirley" were all wild for this lover who, though promised by all the laws of nature and romance, did not appear. They leaned out of their windows, they stretched forth their hands, calling for him— appealing to heaven and earth. Why were they left to wear out their bloom, to lose their freshness, to spend their days in sewing and dreaming, when he, it was certain, was about somewhere, and by sheer perversity of fate could not find the way to them? Nothing was thought of the extra half-million of women in those days; perhaps it had not begun to exist; but that "nobody was coming to marry us, nobody coming to woo" was apparent.

Young ladies like Miss Charlotte Brontë and Miss Ellen Nussey her friend, would have died rather than give vent to such sentiments; but when the one of them to whom that gift was given found that her pen had become a powerful instrument in her hand, the current of the restrained feeling burst all boundaries, and she poured forth the cry which nobody had suspected before. It had been a thing to be denied, to be indignantly contradicted as impossible, if ever a lovesick girl put herself forth to the shame of her fellows and the laugh of the world. When such a phenomenon appeared, she was condemned as either bad or foolish by every law: and the idea that she was capable of "running after" a man was the most dreadful accusation that could be brought against a woman. Miss Brontë's heroines, however, did not precisely do this. Shirley and Caroline Helstone were not in love so much as longing for love, clamouring for it, feeling it to be their right of which they were somehow defrauded. There is a good deal to be said for such a view. If it is the most virtuous thing in the world for a man to desire to marry, to found a family, to be the father of children, it should be no shameful thing for a woman to own the same desire. But it is somehow against the instinct of primitive humanity, which has decided that the woman should be no more than responsive, maintaining a reserve in respect to her feelings, subduing the expression, unless in the "once, and only once, and to One only" of the poet.

Charlotte Brontë was the first to overthrow this superstition. Personally I am disposed to stand for the superstition, and dislike all transgression of it. But that was not the view of the most reticent and self-controlled of maidens, the little governess, clad in all the strict proprieties of the period, the parson's daughter despising curates, and unacquainted with other men. In her secret heart, she demanded of fate night and day why she, so full of life and capability, should be left there to dry up and wither; and why Providence refused her the completion of her being. Her heart was not set on a special love; still less was there anything fleshly or sensual in her imagination. It is a shame to use such words in speaking of her, even though to cast them forth as wholly inapplicable. The woman's grievance—that she should be left there unwooed, unloved, out of reach of the natural openings of life: without hope of motherhood: with the great instinct of her being unfulfilled—was almost a philosophical, and entirely an abstract, grievance, felt by her for her kind: for every woman dropped out of sight and unable to attain the manner of existence for which she was created. And I think it was the first time this cry had been heard out of the mouth of a perfectly modest and pure-minded woman, nay, out of the mouth of any woman; for it had nothing to do with the shriek of the Sapphos for love. It was more startling, more confusing to the general mind, than the wail of the lovelorn. The gentle victim of "a disappointment," or even the soured and angered victim, was a thing quite understood and familiar: but not the woman calling upon heaven and earth to witness that all the fates were conspiring against her to cheat her of her natural career.

So far as I can see this was the great point which gave force to Charlotte Brontë's genius and conferred upon her the curious pre-eminence she possesses among the romancers of her time. In this view "Shirley," though I suppose the least popular, is the most characteristic of her works. It is dominated throughout with this complaint. Curates? Yes, there they are, a group of them. Is that the thing you expect us women to marry? Yet it is our right to bear children, to guide the house. And we are half of the world, and where is the provision for us?

This cry disturbed the critic, the reader, the general public in the most curious way; they did not know what to make of it. Was it a shameless woman who was so crying out? It is always the easiest way, and one which avoids all complications, to say so, and thus crush every question. But it was scarcely easy to believe this in face of other circumstances. Mrs. Gaskell, as much puzzled as any one, when Charlotte Brontë's short life was over, tried hard to account for it by "environment" as the superior persons say, that is by the wicked folly of her brother, and the coarseness of all the Yorkshiremen round; and thus originated in her bewilderment, let us hope without other intention, a new kind of biography, as the subject of it inaugurated an entirely new kind of social revolution. The cry of the women indeed almost distressed as well as puzzled the world. The vivid genius still held it, but the ideas were alarming, distracting beyond measure. The *Times* blew a trumpet of dismay; the book was revolution as well as revelation. It was an outrage upon good taste, it was a betrayal of sentiments too widespread to be comfortable. It was indelicate if not immodest. We have outgrown now the very use of this word, but it was a potent one at that period. And it was quite a just reproach. That cry shattered indeed altogether the "delicacy" which was supposed to be the most exquisite characteristic of womankind. The softening veil is blown away, when such exhibitions of feeling are given to the world.

From that period to this is a long step. We have travelled

through many years and many gradations of sentiment: and we have now arrived at a standard of opinion by which the "sex-problem" has become the most interesting of questions, the chief occupation of fiction, to be discussed by men and women alike with growing warmth and openness, the immodest and the indelicate being equally and scornfully dismissed as barriers with which Art has nothing to do. My impression is that Charlotte Brontë was the pioneer and founder of this school of romance, though it would probably have shocked and distressed her as much as any other woman of her age.

* * * * *

The novels of Emily and Anne Brontë were published shortly after "Jane Eyre," in three volumes, of which "Wuthering Heights" occupied the first two. I am obliged to confess that I have never shared the common sentiment of enthusiasm for that, to me, unlovely book. The absence of almost every element of sympathy in it, the brutality and misery, tempered only by an occasional gleam of the heather, the freshness of an occasional blast over the moors, have prevented me from appreciating a force which I do not deny but cannot admire. The figure of Heathcliffe, which perhaps has called forth more praise than any other single figure in the literature of the time, does not touch me. I can understand how in the jumble which the reader unconsciously makes, explaining him more or less by Rochester and other of Charlotte Brontë's heroes, he may take his place in a sort of system, and thus have humanities read into him, so to speak, which he does not himself possess. But though the horror and isolation of the house is powerful I have never been able to reconcile myself either to the story or treatment, or to the estimate of Emily Brontë's genius held so strongly by so many people. There is perhaps the less harm in refraining from much comment on this singular book, of which I gladly admit the unique character, since it has been the occasion of so many and such enthusiastic comments. To me Emily Brontë is chiefly interesting as the double of her sister, exaggerating at once and softening her character and genius as showing those limits of superior sense and judgment which restrained her, and the softer lights which a better developed humanity threw over the landscape common to them both. We perceive better the tempering sense of possibility by which Charlotte made her rude and almost brutal hero still attractive, even in his masterful ferocity, when we see Emily's incapacity to express anything in *her* hero except perhaps a touch of that tragic pathos, prompting to fiercer harshness still, which is in the soul of a man who never more, whatever he does, can set himself right. This is the one strain of poetry to my mind in the wild conception. There was no measure in the younger sister's thoughts, nor temperance in her methods.

The youngest of all, the gentle Anne, would have no right to be considered at all as a writer but for her association with these imperative spirits. An ordinary little novelette and a moral story, working out the disastrous knowledge gained by acquaintance with the unfortunate Branwell's ruinous habits, were her sole productions. She was the element wanting in Emily's rugged work and nature. Instead of being two sisters constantly entwined with each other, never separate when they could help it, had Anne been by some fantastic power swamped altogether and amalgamated with her best beloved, we may believe that Emily might then have shown herself the foremost of the three. But the group as it stands is more interesting than any single individual could be. And had Charlotte Brontë lived a long and triumphant life, a fanciful writer might have imagined that the throwing off of those other threads of being so closely attached to her own had poured greater force and charity into her veins. But we are baffled in all our suggestions for the amendment of the ways of Providence.

* * * * *

The melancholy and tragic year, or rather six months, which swept from Haworth Parsonage three of its inmates, and left Charlotte and her father alone to face life as they might, was now approaching; and it seems so completely an episode in the story of the elder sister's genius as well as her life, that its history is like that of an unwritten tragedy, hers as much as her actual work. Branwell was the first to die, unwept yet not without leaving a pathetic note in the record. Then came the extraordinary passion and agony of Emily, which has affected the imagination so much, and which, had it been for any noble purpose, would have been a true martyrdom. But to die the death of a Stoic, in fierce resistance yet subjection to Nature, regardless of the feelings of all around, for the sake of pride and self-will alone, is not an act to be looked upon with the reverential sympathy which, however, it has secured from many. The strange creature with her shoes on her feet and her staff in her hand, refusing till the last to acknowledge herself to be ill or to receive any help in her weakness, gives thus a kind of climax to her strange and painful work. Her death took place in December of the same year (1848) in which Branwell died. Anne, already delicate, would never seem to have held up her head after her sister's death, and in May 1849 she followed, but in all sweetness and calmness, to her early grave. She was twenty-eight; Emily twenty-nine. So soon had the fever of life worn itself out and peace come. Charlotte was left alone. There had not been to her in either of them the close companion which they had found in each other. But yet life ebbed away from her with their deaths, which occurred in such a startling and quick succession as always makes bereavement more terrible.

This occurred at the height of her mental activity. "Shirley" had been published, and had been received with the divided feeling we have referred to; and when she was thus left alone she found, no doubt, the solace which of all mortal things work gives best, by resuming her natural occupation in the now more than ever sombre seclusion of the Parsonage, to which, however, her favourite friend, Ellen Nussey, came from time to time. One or two visits to London occurred after the two first publications in which, a demure little person, silent and shy, yet capable of expressing herself very distinctly by times, and by no means unconscious of the claim she now had upon other people's respect and admiration, Charlotte Brontë made a little sensation in the society which was opened to her, not always of a very successful kind. Everybody will remember the delightfully entertaining chapter in literary history in which Mrs. Ritchie, with charming humour and truth, recounts the visit of this odd little lion to her father's house, and Thackeray's abrupt and clandestine flight to his club when it was found that nothing more was to be made of her than an absorbed conversation with the governess in the back drawing-room, a situation like one in a novel, and so very like the act of modest greatness, singling out the least important person as the object of her attentions.

She is described by all her friends as plain, even ugly—a small woman with a big nose, and no other notable feature, not even the bright eyes which are generally attributed to genius—which was probably, however, better than the lackadaisical portrait prefixed to her biography, after a picture by Richmond, which is the typical portrait of a governess of the old style, a gentle creature deprecating and wistful. Her letters are very good letters, well expressed in something of the old-fashioned way, but without any of the charm of a born letter-writer. Indeed, charm does not seem to have been hers in any way. But she had a few very staunch friends who held fast by her all her life, notwithstanding the uncomfortable experience of being "put in a book," which few people like. It is a gift by itself to put other living people in books. The novelist does not always possess it; to many the realms of imagination are far more easy than the arid realms of fact, and to frame an image of a man much more natural than to take his portrait. I am not sure that it is not a mark of greater strength to be able to put a living and recognisable person on the canvas than it is to invent one. Anyhow, Miss Brontë possessed it in great perfection. Impossible to doubt that the characters of "Shirley" were real men; still more impossible to doubt for a moment the existence of M. Paul Emmanuel. The pursuit of such a system requires other faculties than those of the mere romancist. It demands a very clear-cut opinion, a keen judgment not disturbed by any strong sense of the complexities of nature, nor troubled by any possibility of doing injustice to its victim.

* * * * *

One thing strikes us very strongly in the description of the school, Lowood, which was her very first step in literature, and in which there can now be no doubt, from her own remarks on the manner in which it was received, she had a vindictive purpose. I scarcely know why, for, of course, the dates are all there to prove the difference—but my own conclusion had always been that she was a girl of fourteen or fifteen, old enough to form an opinion when she left the school. I find, with much consternation, that she was only nine; and that so far as such a strenuous opinion was her own at all, it must have been formed at that early and not very judicious age. That the picture should be so vivid with only a little girl's recollection to go upon is wonderful; but it is not particularly valuable as a verdict against a great institution, its founder and all its ways. Nevertheless, it had its scathing and wounding effect as much as if thelittle observer, whose small judgment worked so precociously, had been capable of understanding the things which she condemned. It would be rash to trust nineteen in such a report, but nine!

It was at a different age and in other circumstances that Charlotte Brontë made her deep and extraordinary study of the Brussels Pensionnat. She was twenty-seven; she had already gone through a number of those years of self-repression during which, by dint of keeping silence, the heart burns. She was, if we may accept the freedom of her utterances in fiction as more descriptive of her mind than the measured sentences of her letters, angry with fate and the world which denied her a brighter career, and bound her to the cold tasks of dependence and the company of despised and almost hated inferiors during the best of her life. Her tremendous gift of sight—not second sight or any visionary way of regarding the object before her, but that vivid and immediate vision which took in every detail, and was decisive on every act as if it had been the vision of the gods— was now fully matured. She saw all that was about her with this extraordinary clearness without any shadow upon the object or possibility of doubt as to her power of seeing it all round and through and through. She makes us also see and know the big white house, with every room distinct: the garden, with its great trees and alleys: the class-rooms, each with its tribune: the girls, fat and round and phlegmatic in characteristic foreignism, and herself as spectator, looking on with contemptuous indifference, not caring to discriminate between them. The few English figures, which concern her more, are drawn keen upon the canvas, though with as little friendliness; the teachers sharply accentuated, Mdlle. Sophie, for instance, who, when she is in a rage, has no lips, and all the sharp contentions and false civilities of those banded Free Lances, enemies to everybody and to each other; the image of watchful suspicion in the head of the house—all these are set forth in glittering lines of steel. There is not a morsel of compunction in the picture. Everybody is bad, worthless, a hater of the whole race. The mistress of the establishment moves about stealthily, watching, her eyes showing through a mist in every corner, going and coming without a sound. What a picture it is! There is not a good meaning in the whole place—not even that beneficent absence of meaning which softens the view. They are all bent on their own aims, on gaining an advantage great or small over their neighbours; nobody is spared, nobody is worth a revision of judgment—except one.

The little Englishwoman herself, who is the centre of all

this, is not represented as more lovable than the rest. She is the hungry little epicure, looking on while others feast, and envying every one of them, even while she snarls at their fare as apples of Gomorrah. She cannot abide that they should be better off than she, even though she scorns their satisfaction in what they possess. Her wild and despairing rush through Brussels when the town is *en fête*, cold, impassioned, fever-hot with rancour and loneliness, produces the most amazing effect on the mind. She is the banished spirit for whom there is no place, the little half-tamed wild beast, wild with desire to tear and rend everything that is happy. One feels that she has a certain justification and realises the full force of being left out in the cold, of having no part or lot in the matter when other people are amused and rejoice. Many other writers have endeavoured to produce a similar effect with milder means, but I suppose because of a feeble-minded desire to preserve the reputation of their forlorn heroine and give the reader an amiable view of her, no one has succeeded like the author of "Villette," who is in no way concerned for the amiability of Lucy Snowe.

For the impartiality of this picture is as extraordinary as its power. Lucy Snowe is her own historian; it is the hot blood of the autobiographist that rushes through her veins, yet no attempt is made to recommend her to the reader or gain his sympathy. She is much too real to think of these outside things, or of how people will judge her, or how to make her proceedings acceptable to their eyes. We do not know whether Charlotte Brontë ever darted out of the white still house, standing dead in the moonlight, and rushed through the streets and, like a ghost, into the very heart of the gaslights and festivities; but it would be difficult to persuade any reader that some one had not done so, imprinting that phantasmagoria of light and darkness upon a living brain. Whether it was Charlotte Brontë or Lucy Snowe, the effect is the same. We are not even asked to feel for her or pity her, much less to approve her. Nothing is demanded from us on her account but merely to behold the soul in revolt and the strange workings of her despair. It was chiefly because of the indifference to her of Dr. John that Lucy was thus driven into a momentary madness; and with the usual regardless indiscretion of all Charlotte Brontë's amateur biographers, Mr. Shorter intimates to us who was the living man who was Dr. John and occasioned all the commotion. The tragedy, however it appears, was unnecessary, for the victim got over it with no great difficulty, and soon began the much more engrossing interest which still remained behind.

Nothing up to this point has attracted us in "Villette," except, indeed, the tremendous vitality and reality of the whole, the sensation of the actual which is in every line, and which forbids us to believe for a moment that what we are reading is fiction. But a very different sentiment comes into being as we become acquainted with the black bullet-head and vivacious irascible countenance of M. Paul Emmanuel. He is the one only character in Miss Brontë's little world who has a real charm, whose entrance upon the stage warms all our feelings and awakens in us not interest alone, but lively liking, amusement and sympathy. The quick-witted, quick-tempered Frenchman, with all the foibles of his vanity displayed, as susceptible to any little slight as a girl, as easily pleased with a sign of kindness, as far from the English ideal as it is possible to imagine, dancing with excitement, raging with displeasure, committing himself by every step he takes, cruel, delightful, barbarous and kind, is set before us in the fullest light, intolerable but always enchanting. He is as full of variety as Rosalind, as devoid of dignity as Pierrot, contradictory, inconsistent, vain, yet conquering all our prejudices and enchanting us while he performs every antic that, according to our usual code, a man ought not to be capable of. How was it that for this once the artist got the better of all her restrictions and overcame all her misconceptions, and gave us a man to be heartily loved, laughed at, and taken into our hearts?

I cannot answer that question. I am sorry that he was M. Héger, and the master of the establishment, and not the clever tutor who had so much of Madame Beck's confidence. But anyhow, he is the best that Miss Brontë ever did for us, the most attractive individual, the most perfect picture. The Rochesters were all more or less fictitious, notwithstanding the unconscious inalienable force of realism which gives them, in spite of themselves and us, a kind of overbearing life; but Miss Brontë never did understand what she did not know. She had to see a thing before it impressed itself upon her, and when she did see it, with what force she saw! She knew M. Paul Emmanuel, watching him day by day, seeing all his littlenesses and childishness, his vanity, his big warm heart, his clever brain, the manifold nature of the man. He stands out, as the curates stood out, absolutely real men about whom we could entertain no doubt, recognisable anywhere. The others were either a woman's men, like the Moors of Shirley, whose roughness was bluster (she could not imagine an Englishman who was not rough and rude), and their strength more or less made up; or an artificial composition like St. John, an ideal bully like Rochester. The ideal was not her forte—she had few gifts that way: but she saw with overwhelming lucidity and keenness, and what she saw, without a doubt, without a scruple, she could put upon the canvas in lines of fire. Seldom, very seldom, did an object appear within reach of that penetrating light, which could be drawn lovingly or made to appear as a being to be loved. Was not the sole model of that species M. Paul? It would seem that in the piteous poverty of her life, which was so rich in natural power, she had never met before a human creature in whom she could completely trust, or one who commended himself to her entirely, with all his foibles and weaknesses increasing, not diminishing, the charm.

It is, in my opinion, a most impertinent inquiry to endeavour to search out what were the sentiments of Charlotte Brontë for M. Héger. Any one whom it would be more impossible to imagine as breaking the very first rule of English decorum, and letting her thoughts stray towards another woman's husband, I cannot imagine. Her fancy was wild and her utterance free, and she liked to think that men were quite untrammelled by those proprieties which bound herself like bonds of iron in her private person, and that she might pluck a fearful joy by listening to their dreadful experiences: but she herself was as prim and Puritan as any little blameless governess that ever went out of an English parish. But while believing this I cannot but feel it was an intolerable spite of fortune that the one manwhom she knew in her life, whom her story could make others love, the only man whom she saw with that real illumination which does justice to humanity, was not M. Paul Emmanuel but M. Héger. This was why we were left trembling at the end of Lucy Snowe's story, not knowing whether he ever came back to her out of the wilds, fearing almost as keenly that nothing but loss could fitly end the tale, yet struggling in our imaginations against the doom—as if it had concerned our own happiness.

Was this new-born power in her, the power of representing a man at his best, she who by nature saw both men and women from their worst side, a sign of the development of genius in herself, the softening of that scorn with which she had hitherto regarded a world chiefly made up of inferior beings, the mellowing influence of maturity? So we might have said, had it not been that after this climax of production she never spake word more in the medium of fiction. Had she told the world everything she had to say? Could she indeed say nothing but what she had seen and known in her limited experience— the trials of school and governessing, the longing of women, the pangs of solitude? That strange form of imagination which can deal only with fact, and depict nothing but what is under its eyes, is in its way perhaps the most impressive of all—especially when inspired by the remorseless lights of that keen outward vision which is unmitigated by any softening of love for the race, any embarrassing toleration as to feelings and motives. It is unfortunately true in human affairs that those who expect a bad ending to everything, and suspect a motive at least dubious to every action, prove right in a great number of cases, and that the qualities of truth and realism have been appropriated to their works by almost universal consent. Indeed there are some critics who think this the only true form of art. But it is at the same time a power with many limitations. The artist who labours, as M. Zola does, searching into every dust-heap, as if he could find out human nature, the only thing worth depicting, with all its closely hidden secrets, all its flying indistinguishable tones, all its infinite gradations of feeling, by that nauseous process, or by a roaring progress through the winds, upon a railway brake, or the visit of a superficial month to the most complicated, the most subtle of cities—must lay up for himself and for his reader many disappointments and deceptions: but the science of artistic study, as exemplified in him, had not been invented in Charlotte Brontë's day.

She did not attempt to go and see things with the intention of representing them; she was therefore limited to the representation of those things which naturally in the course of life came under her eyes. She knew, though only as a child, the management and atmosphere of a great school, and set it forth, branding a great institution with an insufferable stigma, justly or unjustly, who knows? She went to another school and turned out every figure in it for our inspection—a community all jealous, spiteful, suspicious, clandestine: even the chance pupil with no particular relation to her story or herself, painted with all her frivolities for the edification of the world did not escape. "She was Miss So-and-So," say the army of commentators who have followed Miss Brontë, picking up all the threads, so that the grand-daughter of the girl who had the misfortune to be in the Brussels Pensionnat along with that remorseless artist may be able to study the character of her ancestress. The public we fear loves this kind of art, however, notwithstanding all its drawbacks.

On the other hand probably no higher inspiration could have set before us so powerfully the image of M. Paul. Thus we are made acquainted with the best and the worst which can be effected by this method—the base in all their baseness, the excellent all the dearer for their characteristic faults: but the one representation scarcely less offensive than the other to the victim. Would it be less trying to the individual to be thus caught, identified, written out large in the light of love and glowing adoration, than in the more natural light of scorn? I know not indeed which would be the worst ordeal to go through, to be drawn like Madame Beck, suspicious, stealthy, with watchful eyes appearing out of every corner, surprising every incautious word, than to be put upon the scene in the other manner, with all your peccadilloes exposed in the light of admiration and fondness, and yourself put to play the part of hero and lover. The point of view of the public is one thing, that of the victim quite another. We are told that Miss Brontë, perhaps with a momentary compunction for what she had done, believed herself to have prevented all injurious effects by securing that "Villette" should not be published in Brussels, or translated into the French tongue, both of them of course perfectly futile hopes since the very desire to hinder its appearance was a proof that this appearance would be of unusual interest. The fury of the lady exposed in all her stealthy ways could scarcely have been less than the confusion of her spouse when he found himself held up to the admiration of his town as Lucy Snowe's captivating lover. To be sure it may be said the public has nothing to do with this. These individuals are dead and gone, and no exposure can hurt them any longer, whereas the gentle reader lives for ever, and goes on through the generations, handing on to posterity his delight in M. Paul. But all the same it is a cruel and in reality an immoral art; and it has this great disadvantage, that its area is extremely circumscribed, especially when the artist lives most of her life in a Yorkshire parsonage amid the moors, where so few notable persons come in her way.

* * * * *

There was however one subject of less absolute realism which Charlotte Brontë had at her command, having experienced in her own person and seen her nearest friends under the experience, of that solitude and longing of women, of which she has made so remarkable an exposition. The long silence of life without an adventure or a change, the forlorn gaze out at windows which never show any one coming who can rouse the slightest interest in the mind, the endless years and days which pass and pass, carrying away the bloom, extinguishing the lights of youth, bringing a dreary middle age before which the very soul shrinks, while yet the sufferer feels how strong is the current of life in her own veins, and how capable she is of all the active duties of existence—this was the essence and soul of the existence she knew best. Was there no help for it? Must the women wait and long and see their lives thrown away, and have no power to save themselves?

The position in itself so tragic is one which can scarcely be expressed without calling forth an inevitable ridicule, a laugh at the best, more often a sneer at the women whose desire for a husband is thus betrayed. Shirley and Caroline Helston both cried out for that husband with an indignation, a fire and impatience, a sense of wrong and injury, which stopped the laugh for the moment. It might be ludicrous but it was horribly genuine and true. Note there was nothing sensual about these young women. It was life they wanted; they knew nothing of the grosser thoughts which the world with its jeers attributes to them: of such thoughts they were unconscious in a primitive innocence which perhaps only women understand. They wanted their life, their place in the world, the rightful share of women in the scheme of nature. Why did not it come to them? The old patience in which women have lived for all the centuries fails now and again in a keen moment of energy when some one arises who sees no reason why she should endure this forced inaction, or why she should invent for herself inferior ways of working and give up her birthright, which is to carry on the world.

The reader was horrified with these sentiments from the lips of young women. The women were half ashamed, yet more than

half stirred and excited by the outcry, which was true enough
if indelicate. All very well to talk of women working for their
living, finding new channels for themselves, establishing their
independence. How much have we said of all that, endeavouring
to persuade ourselves! Charlotte Brontë had the courage of
her opinions. It was not education nor a trade that her women
wanted. It was not a living but their share in life, a much more
legitimate object had that been the way to secure it, or had there
been any way to secure it in England. Miss Brontë herself said
correct things about the protection which a trade is to a woman,
keeping her from a mercenary marriage; but this was not in
the least the way of her heroines. They wanted to be happy, no
doubt, but above all things they wanted their share in life—to
have their position by the side of men, which alone confers a
natural equality, to have their shoulder to the wheel, their hands
on the reins of common life, to build up the world, and link the
generations each to each. In her philosophy marriage was the
only state which procured this, and if she did not recommend
a mercenary marriage she was at least very tolerant about its
conditions, insisting less upon love than was to be expected and
with a covert conviction in her mind that if not one man then
another was better than any complete abandonment of the larger
path. Lucy Snowe for a long time had her heart very much set
on Dr. John and his placid breadth of Englishism: but when she
finally found out that to be impossible her tears were soon dried
by the prospect of Paul Emmanuel, so unlike him, coming into
his place.

Poor Charlotte Brontë! She has not been as other women,
protected by the grave from all betrayal of the episodes in her
own life. Everybody has betrayed her, and all she thought about
this one and that, and every name that was ever associated with
hers. There was a Mr. Taylor from London about whom she wrote
with great freedom to her friend Miss Nussey, telling how the
little man had come, how he had gone away without any advance
in the affairs, how a chill came over her when he appeared and

she found him much less attractive than when at a distance, yet how she liked it as little when he went away and was somewhat excited about his first letter, and even went so far as to imagine with a laugh that there might be possibly a dozen little Joe Taylors before all was over. She was hard upon Miss Austen for having no comprehension of passion, but no one could have been cooler and less impassioned than she as she considered the question of Mr. Taylor, reluctant to come to any decision yet disappointed when it came to nothing. There was no longing in her mind for Mr. Taylor, but there was for life and action and the larger paths and the little Joes.

This longing which she expressed with so much vehemence and some poetic fervour as the burden of the lives of Shirley and her friends has been the keynote of a great deal that has followed—the revolts and rebellions, the wild notions about marriage, the "Sex Problem," and a great deal more. From that first point to the prevailing discussion of all the questions involved is a long way; but it is a matter of logical progression, and when once the primary matter is opened, every enlargement of the subject may be taken as a thing to be expected. Charlotte Brontë was in herself the embodiment of all old-fashioned restrictions. She was proper, she was prim, her life was hedged in by all the little rules which bind the primitive woman. But when she left her little recluse behind and rushed into the world of imagination her exposure of the bondage in which she sat with all her sisters was far more daring than if she had been a woman of many experiences and knew what she was speaking of. She did know the longing, the discontent, the universal contradiction and contrariety which is involved in that condition of unfulfilment to which so many grey and undeveloped lives are condemned. For her and her class, which did not speak of it, everything depended upon whether the woman married or did not marry. Their thoughts were thus artificially fixed to one point in the horizon, but their ambition was neither ignoble nor unclean. It was bold, indeed, in proportion to its almost ridiculous innocence, and want of perception of any grosser side. Their share in life, their part in the mutual building of the house, was what they sought. But the seed she thus sowed has come to many growths which would have appalled Charlotte Brontë. Those who took their first inspiration from this cry of hers, have quite forgotten what it was she wanted, which was not emancipation but an extended duty. But while it would be very unjust to blame her for the vagaries that have followed and to which nothing could be less desirable than any building of the house or growth of the race, any responsibility or service—we must still believe that it was she who drew the curtain first aside and opened the gates to imps of evil meaning, polluting and profaning the domestic hearth.

The marriage which—after all these wild embodiments of the longing and solitary heart which could not consent to abandon its share in life, after Shirley and Lucy Snowe, and that complex unity of three female souls all unfulfilled, which had now been broken by death—she accepted in the end of her life, is the strangest commentary upon all that went before, or rather, upon all the literary and spiritual part of her history, though it was a quite appropriate ending to Mr. Brontë's daughter, and even to the writer of those sober letters which discussed Mr. Taylor, whether he should or should not be encouraged, and how it was a little disappointing after all to see him go away. Her final suitor was one of the class which she had criticised so scathingly, one who, it might have been thought, would scarcely have ventured to enter the presence or brave the glance of so penetrating an eye, but who would seem to have brought all the urgency of a *grand passion* to the sombre parlour of the parsonage, to the afternoon stillness of the lonely woman who would not seem to have suspected anything of the kind till it was poured out before her without warning. She was startled and confused by his declaration and appeal, never apparently having contemplated the possibility of any such occurrence; and in the interval which followed the father raged and resisted, and the lover did not conceal his heartbroken condition but suffered without complaining while the lady looked on wistful, touched and attracted by the unlooked-for love, and gradually melting towards that, though indifferent to the man who offered it. Mr. Brontë evidently thought that if this now distinguished daughter who had been worshipped among the great people in London, and talked of in all the newspapers, married at all in her mature age, it should be some one distinguished like herself, and not the mere curate who was the natural fate of every clergyman's daughter, the simplest and least known.

Charlotte meanwhile said no word, but saw the curate enact various tragic follies of love for her sake with a sort of awe and wonder, astonished to find herself thus possessed still of the charm which none are so sure as women that only youth and beauty can be expected to possess. And she had never had any beauty, and, though she was not old, was no longer young. It is a conventional fiction that a woman still in the thirties is beyond the exercise of that power. Indeed, it would be hard to fix the age at which the spell departs. Certainly the demeanour of Mr. Nicholls gave her full reason to believe that it had not departed from her. He faltered in the midst of the service, grew pale, almost lost his self-possession when he suddenly saw her among the kneeling figures round the altar; and no doubt this rather shocking and startling exhibition of his feelings was more pardonable to the object of so much emotion than it was likely to have been to any other spectator. The romance is a little strange, but yet it is a romance in its quaint ecclesiastical way. And soon Charlotte was drawn still more upon her lover's side by the violence of her father. It was decided that the curate was to go, and that this late gleam of love-making was to be extinguished and the old dim atmosphere to settle down again for ever. Finally, however, the mere love of love, which had always been more to her than any personal inclination, and the horror of that permanent return to the twilight of dreamy living against which she had struggled all her life, overcame her, and gave her courage; but she married characteristically, not as women marry who are carried to a new home and make a new beginning in life, but retaining all the circumstances of the old and receiving her husband into her father's house where she had already passed through so many fluctuations and dreamed so many dreams, and which was full to overflowing with the associations of the past.

We have no reason to suppose that it did not add to the happiness of her life; indeed, every indication is to the contrary, and the husband seems to have been kind, considerate and affectionate. Still this thing upon which so many of her thoughts had been fixed during her whole life, which she had felt to be the necessary condition of full development, and for which the little impassioned female circle of which she was the expositor had sighed and cried to heaven and earth, came to her at last very much in the form of a catastrophe. No doubt the circumstances of her quickly failing health and shortened life promote this feeling. But without really taking these into consideration the sensation remains the same. The strange little keen soul with its sharply fixed restrictions, yet intense force of perception within its limits, dropped out of the world into which it had made an irruption so brilliant and so brief and sank out of sight altogether, sank into the humdrum house between the old father and the sober husband, into the clerical atmosphere with which she had no sympathy, into the absolute quiet of domestic life to which no Prince Charming could now come gaily round the corner, out of the mists and moors, and change with a touch of his wand the grey mornings and evenings into golden days. Well! was not this that which she had longed for, the natural end of life towards which her Shirley, her Caroline, her Lucy had angrily stretched forth their hands, indignant to be kept waiting, clamouring for instant entrance? And so it was, but how different! Lucy Snowe's little housekeeping, all the preparations which M. Paul made for her comfort and which seemed better to her than any palace, would not they too have taken the colour of perpetual dulness if everything had settled down and the Professor assumed his slippers by the domestic hearth? Ah no, for Lucy Snowe loved the man, and Charlotte Brontë, as appears, loved only the love. It is a parable. She said a little later that she began to see that this was the fate which she would wish for those she loved best, for her friend Ellen, perhaps for her Emily if she had lived—the good man very faithful, very steady, worth his weight in gold— yet flatter than the flattest days of old, *solidement nourri*, a good substantial husband, managing all the parish business, full of talk about the Archdeacon's charge, and the diocesan meetings, and the other clergy of the moorland parishes. We can conceive that she got to fetching his slippers for him and taking great care that he was comfortable, and perhaps had it been so ordained might have grown into a contented matron and forgotten the glories and miseries, so inseparably twined and linked together, of her youth. But she only had a year in which to do all that, and this is how her marriage seems to turn into a catastrophe, the caging of a wild creature that had never borne captivity before, and which now could no longer rush forth into the heart of any shining *fête*, or to the window of a strange confessional, anywhere, to throw off the burden of the perennial contradiction, the ceaseless unrest of the soul, the boilings of the volcano under the snow.

* * * * *

I have said it was difficult to account for the extreme interest still attaching to everything connected with Charlotte Brontë; not only the story of her peculiar genius, but also of everybody connected with her, though the circle was in reality quite a respectable, humdrum, and uninteresting one, containing nobody of any importance except the sister, who was her own wilder and fiercer part. One way, however, in which these sisters have won some part of their long-lasting interest is due to the treatment to which they have been subjected. They are the first victims of that ruthless art of biography which is one of the features of our time; and that not only by Mrs. Gaskell, who took up her work in something of an apologetic vein, and was so anxious to explain how it was that her heroine expressed certain ideas not usual in the mouths of women, that she was compelled to take away the reputation of a number of other people in order to excuse the peculiarities of these two remarkable women. But everybody who has touched their history since, and there have been many—for it would seem that gossip, when restrained by no bonds of decorum or human feeling, possesses a certain interest whether it is concerned with the household of a cardinal or that of a parish priest—has followed the same vicious way without any remonstrance or appeal for mercy. We have all taken it for granted that no mercy was to be shown to the Brontës. Let every rag be torn from Charlotte, of whom there is the most to say. Emily had the good luck to be no correspondent, and so has escaped to some degree the complete exposure of every confidence and every thought which has happened to her sister. Is it because she has nobody to defend her that she has been treated thus barbarously? I cannot conceive a situation more painful, more lacerating to every feeling, than that of the father and the husband dwelling silent together in that sombre parsonage, from which every ray of light seems to depart with the lost woman, whose presence had kept a little savour in life, and looking on in silence to see their life taken to pieces, and every decent veil dragged from the inner being of their dearest and nearest. They complained as much as two voiceless persons could, or at least the father complained: and the very servants came hot from their kitchen to demand a vindication of their character: but nobody noted the protest of the old man amid the silence of the moors: and the husband was more patient and spoke no word. Even he, however, after nearly half a century, when that far-off episode of life must have become dim to him, has thrown his relics open for a little more revelation, a little more interference with the helpless ashes of the dead.

No dot is now omitted upon i, no t left uncrossed. We know, or at least are told, who Charlotte meant by every character she ever portrayed, even while the model still lives. We know her opinion of her friends, or rather acquaintances, the people whom she saw cursorily and formed a hasty judgment upon, as we all do in the supposed safety of common life. Protests have been offered in other places against a similar treatment of other persons; but scarcely any protest has been attempted in respect to Charlotte Brontë. The resurrection people have been permitted to make their researches as they pleased. It throws a curious pathos, a not unsuitably tragic light upon a life always so solitary, that this should all have passed in silence because there was actually no one to interfere, no one to put a ban upon the dusty heaps and demand that no mere should be said. When one looks into the matter a little more closely, one finds it is so with almost all those who have specially suffered at the hands of the biographer. The Carlyles had no child, no brother to rise up in their defence. It gives the last touch of melancholy to the conclusion of a lonely life. Mrs. Gaskell, wise woman, defended herself from a similar treatment by will, and left children behind her to protect her memory. But the Brontës are at the mercy of every one who cares to give another raking to the diminished heap of *débris*. The last writer who has done so, Mr. Clement Shorter, had some real new light to throw upon a story which surely has now been sufficiently turned inside out, and has done his work withperfect good feeling, and, curiously enough after so many exploitations, in a way which shows that interest has not yet departed from the subject. But we trust that now the memory of Charlotte Brontë will be allowed to rest.

AN EXCERPT FROM
Women Novelists of Queen Victoria's Reign
- A Book of Appreciations, 1897

HAWORTH

BY VIRGINIA WOOLF

Haworth was the home of the Brontë family. Virginia Woolf's account of a visit to Haworth was the first of her writings to be accepted for publication (and the second to appear in print.) Woolf's article was first published in The Guardian, unsigned, on 21st December, 1904.

I do not know whether pilgrimages to the shrines of famous men ought not to be condemned as sentimental journeys. It is better to read Carlyle in your own study chair than to visit the sound-proof room and pore over the manuscripts at Chelsea. I should be inclined to set up an examination on Frederick the Great in place of an entrance fee; only, in that case, the house would soon have to be shut up. The curiosity is only legitimate when the house of a great writer or the country in which it is set adds something to our understanding of his books. This justification you have for a pilgrimage to the home and country of Charlotte Brontë and her sisters.

The *Life*, by Mrs Gaskell, gives you the impression that Haworth and the Brontës are somehow inextricably mixed. Haworth expresses the Brontës; the Brontës express Haworth; they fit like a snail to its shell. How far surroundings radically affect people's minds, it is not for me to ask: superficially, the influence is great, but it is worth asking if the famous parsonage had been placed in a London slum, the dens of Whitechapel would not have had the same result as the lonely Yorkshire moors. However, I am taking away my only excuse for visiting Haworth. Unreasonable or not, one of the chief points of a recent visit to Yorkshire was that an expedition to Haworth could be accomplished. The necessary arrangements were made, and we determined to take advantage of the first day for our expedition. A real northern snowstorm had been doing the honours of the moors. It was rash to wait fine weather, and it was also cowardly. I understand that the sun very seldom shone on the Brontë family, and if we chose a really fine day we should have to make allowance for the fact that fifty years ago there were few fine days at Haworth, and that we were, therefore, for sake of comfort, rubbing out half the shadows on the picture. However, it would be interesting to see what impression Haworth could make upon the brilliant weather of Settle. We certainly passed through a very cheerful land, which might be likened to a vast wedding cake, of which the icing was slightly undulating; the earth was bridal in its virgin snow, which helped to suggest the comparison.

Keighley - pronounced Keethly - is often mentioned in the *Life*; it was the big town four miles from Haworth in which Charlotte walked to make her more important purchases - her wedding gown, perhaps, and the thin little cloth boots which we examined under glass in the Brontë Museum. It is a big manufacturing town, hard and stony, and clattering with business, in the way of these Northern towns. They make small provision for the sentimental traveller, and our only occupation was to picture the slight figure of Charlotte trotting along the streets in her thin mantle, hustled into the gutter by more burly passers-by. It was the Keighley of her day, and that was some comfort. Our excitement as we neared Haworth had in it an element of suspense that was really painful, as though we were to meet some long-separated friend, who might have changed in the interval - so clear an image of Haworth had we from print and picture. At a certain point we entered the valley, up both sides of which the village climbs, and right on the hill-top, looking down over its parish, we saw the famous oblong tower of the church. This marked the shrine at which we were to do homage.

It may have been the effect of a sympathetic imagination, but I think that there were good reasons why Haworth did certainly strike one not exactly as gloomy, but, what is worse for artistic purposes, as dingy and commonplace. The houses, built of yellow-brown stone, date from the early nineteenth century. They climb the moor step by step in little detached strips, some distance apart, so that the town instead of making one compact blot on the landscape has contrived to get a whole stretch into its clutches. There is a long line of houses up the moor-side, which clusters round the church and parsonage with a little clump of trees. At the top the interest for a Brontë lover becomes suddenly intense. The church, the parsonage, the Brontë Museum, the school where Charlotte taught, and the Bull Inn where Branwell drank are all within a stone's throw of each other. The museum is certainly rather a pallid and inanimate collection of objects. An effort ought to be made to keep things out of these mausoleums, but the choice often lies between them and destruction, so that we must be grateful for the care which has preserved much that is, under any circumstances, of deep interest. Here are many autograph letters, pencil drawings, and other documents. But the most touching case - so touching that one hardly feels reverent in one's gaze - is that which contains the little personal relics of the dead woman. The natural fate of such things is to die before the body that wore them, and because these, trifling and transient though they are, have survived, Charlotte Brontë the woman comes to life, and one forgets the chiefly memorable fact that she was a great writer. Her shoes and her thin muslin dress have outlived her. One other object gives a thrill; the little oak stool which Emily carried with her on her solitary moorland tramps, and on which she sat, if not to write, as they say, to think what was probably better than her writing.

The church, of course, save part of the tower, is renewed since Brontë days; but that remarkable churchyard remains. The old edition of the *Life* had on its title-page a little print which struck the keynote of the book; it seemed to be all graves - gravestones stood ranked all round; you walked on a pavement lettered with dead names; the graves had solemnly invaded the garden of the parsonage itself, which was as a little oasis of life in the midst of the dead. This is no exaggeration of the artist's, as we found: the stones seem to start out of the ground at you in tall, upright lines, like and army of silent soldiers. there is no hand's breadth untenanted; indeed, the economy of space is somewhat irreverent. In old days a flagged path, which suggested the slabs of graves, led from the front door of the parsonage to the churchyard without interruption of wall or hedge; the garden was practically the graveyard too; the successors of the Brontës, however, wishing a little space between life and death, planted a hedge and several tall trees, which now cut off the parsonage garden completely. The house itself is precisely the same as it was in Charlotte's day, save that one new wing has been added. It is easy to shut the eye to this, and then you have the square, boxlike parsonage, built of the ugly yellow-brown stone which they quarry from the moors behind, precisely as it was when Charlotte lived and died there. Inside, of course, the changes are many, though not such as to obscure the original shape of the rooms. There is nothing remarkable in a mid-Victorian parsonage, though tenanted by genius, and the only room which awakens curiosity is the kitchen, now used as an ante-room, in which the girls tramped as they conceived their work. One other spot has a certain grim interest - the oblong recess beside the staircase into which Emily drove her bulldog during the famous fight, and pinned him while she pommelled him. It is otherwise a little sparse parsonage, much like others of its kind. It was due to the courtesy of the present incumbent that we were allowed to inspect it; in his place I should often feel inclined to exorcise the three famous ghosts.

One thing only remained: the church in which Charlotte worshipped, was married, and lies buried. The circumference of her life was very narrow. Here, though much is altered, a few things remain to tell of her. The slab which bears the names of the succession of children and of their parents - their births and deaths - strikes the eye first. Name follows name; at very short intervals they died - Maria the mother, Maria the daughter, Elizabeth, Branwell, Emily, Anne, Charlotte, and lastly the old father, who outlived them all. Emily was only thirty years old, and Charlotte but nine years older. 'The sting of death is sin, and the strength of sin is the law, but thanks be to God which giveth us the victory through our Lord Jesus Christ.' That is the inscription which has been placed beneath their names, and with reason; for however harsh the struggle, Emily, and Charlotte above all, fought to victory.

AN EXCERPT FROM
The Guardian, 1904

CHARLOTTE BRONTË

BY G.K. CHESTERTON

Objection is often raised against realistic biography because it reveals so much that is important and even sacred about a man's life. The real objection to it will rather be found in the fact that it reveals about a man the precise points which are unimportant. It reveals and asserts and insists on exactly those things in a man's life of which the man himself is wholly unconscious; his exact class in society, the circumstances of his ancestry, the place of his present location. These are things which do not, properly speaking, ever arise before the human vision. They do not occur to a man's mind; it may be said, with almost equal truth, that they do not occur in a man's life. A man no more thinks about himself as the inhabitant of the third house in a row of Brixton villas than he thinks about himself as a strange animal with two legs. What a man's name was, what his income was, whom he married, where he lived, these are not sanctities; they are irrelevancies.

A very strong case of this is the case of the Brontës. The Brontë is in the position of the mad lady in a country village; her eccentricities form an endless source of innocent conversation to that exceedingly mild and bucolic circle, the literary world. The truly glorious gossips of literature, like Mr. Augustine Birrell and Mr. Andrew Lang, never tire of collecting all the glimpses and anecdotes and sermons and side-lights and sticks and straws which will go to make a Brontë museum. They are the most personally discussed of all Victorian authors, and the limelight of biography has left few darkened corners in the dark old Yorkshire house. And yet the whole of this biographical investigation, though natural and picturesque, is not wholly suitable to the Brontës. For the Brontë genius was above all things deputed to assert the supreme unimportance of externals. Up to that point truth had always been conceived as existing more or less in the novel of manners. Charlotte Brontë electrified the world by showing that an infinitely older and more elemental truth could be conveyed by a novel in which no person, good or bad, had any manners at all. Her work represents the first great assertion that the humdrum life of modern civilisation is a disguise as tawdry and deceptive as the costume of a *bal masqué*. She showed that abysses may exist inside a governess and eternities inside a manufacturer; her heroine is the commonplace spinster, with the dress of merino and the soul of flame. It is significant to notice that Charlotte Brontë, following consciously or unconsciously the great trend of her genius, was the first to take away from the heroine not only the artificial gold and diamonds of wealth and fashion, but even the natural gold and diamonds of physical beauty and grace. Instinctively she felt that the whole of the exterior must be made ugly that the whole of the interior might be made sublime. She chose the ugliest of women in the ugliest of centuries, and revealed within them all the hells and heavens of Dante.

It may, therefore, I think, be legitimately said that the externals of the Brontës' life, though singularly picturesque in themselves, matter less than the externals of almost any other writers. It is interesting to know whether Jane Austen had any knowledge of the lives of the officers and women of fashion whom she introduced into her masterpieces. It is interesting to know whether Dickens had ever seen a shipwreck or been inside a workhouse. For in these authors much of the conviction is conveyed, not always by adherence to facts, but always by grasp of them. But the whole aim and purport and meaning of the work of the Brontës is that the most futile thing in the whole universe is fact. Such a story as "Jane Eyre" is in itself so monstrous a fable that it ought to be excluded from a book of fairy tales. The characters do not do what they ought to do, nor what they would do, nor it might be said, such is the insanity of the atmosphere, not even what they intend to do. The conduct of Rochester is so primevally and superhumanly caddish that Bret Harte in his admirable travesty scarcely exaggerated it. "Then, resuming his usual manner, he threw his boots at my head and withdrew," does perhaps reach to something resembling caricature. The scene in which Rochester dresses up as an old gipsy has something in it which is really not to be found in any other branch of art, except in the end of the pantomime, where the Emperor turns into a pantaloon. Yet, despite this vast nightmare of illusion and morbidity and ignorance of the world, "Jane Eyre" is perhaps the truest book that was ever written. Its essential truth to life sometimes makes one catch one's breath. For it is not true to manners, which are constantly false, or to facts, which are almost always false; it is true to the only existing thing which is true, emotion, the irreducible minimum, the indestructible germ. It would not matter a single straw if a Brontë story were a hundred times more moonstruck and improbable than "Jane Eyre," or a hundred times more moonstruck and improbable than "Wuthering Heights." It would not matter if George Read stood on his head, and Mrs. Read rode on a dragon, if Fairfax Rochester had four eyes and St. John Rivers three legs, the story would still remain the truest story in the world. The typical Brontë character is, indeed, a kind of monster. Everything in him except the essential is dislocated. His hands are on his legs and his feet on his arms, his nose is above his eyes, but his heart is in the right place.

The great and abiding truth for which the Brontë cycle of fiction stands is a certain most important truth about the enduring spirit of youth, the truth of the near kinship between terror and joy. The Brontë heroine, dingily dressed, badly educated, hampered by a humiliating inexperience, a kind of ugly innocence, is yet, by the very fact of her solitude and her gaucherie, full of the greatest delight that is possible to a human being, the delight of expectation, the delight of an ardent and flamboyant ignorance. She serves to show how futile it is of humanity to suppose that pleasure can be attained chiefly by putting on evening dress every evening, and having a box at the theatre every first night. It is not the man of pleasure who has pleasure; it is not the man of the world who appreciates the world. The man who has learnt to do all conventional things perfectly has at the same time learnt to do them prosaically. It is the awkward man, whose evening dress does not fit him, whose gloves will not go on, whose compliments will not come off, who is really full of the ancient ecstasies of youth. He is frightened enough of society actually to enjoy his triumphs. He has that element of fear which is one of the eternal ingredients of joy. This spirit is the central spirit of the Brontë novel. It is the epic of the exhilaration of the shy man. As such it is of incalculable value in our time, of which the curse is that it does not take joy reverently because it does not take it fearfully. The shabby and inconspicuous governess of Charlotte Brontë, with the small outlook and the small creed, had more commerce with the awful and elemental forces which drive the world than a legion of lawless minor poets. She approached the universe with real simplicity, and, consequently, with real fear and delight. She was, so to speak, shy before the multitude of the stars, and in this she had possessed herself of the only force which can prevent enjoyment being as black and barren as routine. The faculty of being shy is the first and the most delicate of the powers of enjoyment. The fear of the Lord is the beginning of pleasure.

Upon the whole, therefore, I think it may justifiably be said that the dark wild youth of the Brontës in their dark wild Yorkshire home has been somewhat exaggerated as a necessary factor in their work and their conception. The emotions with which they dealt were universal emotions, emotions of the morning of existence, the springtide joy and the springtide terror. Every one of us as a boy or girl has had some midnight dream of nameless obstacle and unutterable menace, in which there was, under whatever imbecile forms, all the deadly stress and panic of "Wuthering Heights." Every one of us has had a day-dream of our own potential destiny not one atom more reasonable than "Jane Eyre." And the truth which the Brontës came to tell us is the truth that many waters cannot quench love, and that suburban respectability cannot touch or damp a secret enthusiasm. Clapham, like every other earthly city, is built upon a volcano. Thousands of people go to and fro in the wilderness of bricks and mortar, earning mean wages, professing a mean religion, wearing a mean attire, thousands of women who have never found any expression for their exaltation or their tragedy but to go on working harder and yet harder at dull and automatic employments, at scolding children or stitching shirts. But out of all these silent ones one suddenly became articulate, and spoke a resonant testimony, and her name was Charlotte Brontë. Spreading around us upon every side to-day like a huge and radiating geometrical figure are the endless branches of the great city. There are times when we are almost stricken crazy, as well we may be, by the multiplicity of those appalling perspectives, the frantic arithmetic of that unthinkable population. But this thought of ours is in truth nothing but a fancy. There are no chains of houses; there are no crowds of men. The colossal diagram of streets and houses is an illusion, the opium dream of a speculative builder. Each of these men is supremely solitary and supremely important to himself. Each of these houses stands in the centre of the world. There is no single house of all those millions which has not seemed to someone at some time the heart of all things and the end of travel.

AN EXCERPT FROM
Varied Types, 1905

EMILY BRONTË

BY ARTHUR SYMONS

This was a woman young and passionate,
Loving the Earth, and loving most to be
Where she might be alone with liberty;
Loving the beasts, who are compassionate;
The homeless moors, her home; the bright elate
Winds of the cold dawn; rock and stone and tree;
Night, bringing dreams out of eternity;
And memory of Death's unforgetting date.
She too was unforgetting: has she yet
Forgotten that long agony when her breath
Too fierce for living fanned the flame of death?
Earth for her heather, does she now forget
What pity knew not in her love from scorn,
And that it was an unjust thing to be born?

The Stoic in woman has been seen once only, and that in the only woman in whom there has been seen the paradox of passion without sensuousness. Emily Brontë lived with an unparalleled energy a life of outward quiet, in a loneliness which she shared only with the moors and with the animals whom she loved. She required no passion-experience to endow her with more than a memory of passion. Passion was alive in her as flame is alive in the earth. And the vehemence of that inner fire fed on itself, and wore out her body before its time, because it had no respite and no outlet. We see her condemned to self-imprisonment, and dying of too much life.

Her poems are few and brief, and nothing more personal has ever been written. A few are as masterly in execution as in conception, and almost all have a direct truth of utterance, which rarely lacks at least the bare beauty of muscle and sinew, of a kind of naked strength and alertness. They are without heat or daylight, the sun is rarely in them, and then 'blood-red'; light comes as starshine, or comes as

> Hostile light
> That does not warm but burn.

At times the landscape in this bare, grey, craggy verse, always a landscape of Yorkshire moors, with its touches of stern and tender memory, 'The mute bird sitting on the stone,' 'A little and a lone green lane,' has a quality more thrilling than that of Wordsworth. There is none of his observation, and none of his sense of a benignant 'presence far more deeply interfused'; but there is the voice of the heart's roots, crying out to its home in the earth.

At first this unornamented verse may seem forbidding, may seem even to be ordinary, as an actual moorland may, to those for whom it has no special attraction. But in the verse, as on the moors, there is space, wind, and the smell of the earth; and there is room to be alone, that liberty which this woman cried for when she cried:

> Leave the heart that now I bear,
> And give me liberty.

To be alone was for her to be alone with 'a chainless soul,' which asked of whatever powers might be only 'courage to endure,' constancy not to forget, and the right to leave the door wide open to those visions that came to her out of mere fixed contemplation: 'the God of Visions,' as she called her imagination, 'my slave, my comrade, and my king.' And we know that her courage was flawless, heroic, beyond praise; that she forgot nothing, not even that love for her unspeakable brother, for whom she has expressed in two of her poems a more than masculine magnanimity of pity and contempt; and that at all times she could turn inward to that world within, where her imagination waited for her,

> Where thou, and I, and Liberty
> Have undisputed sovereignty.

Yet even imagination, though 'benignant,' is to her a form of 'phantom bliss' to which she will not trust herself wholly. 'So hopeless is the world without': but is the world within ever quite frankly accepted as a substitute, as a truer reality? She is always on her guard against imagination as against the outer world, whose 'lies' she is resolved shall not 'beguile' her. She has accepted reason as the final arbiter, and desires only to see clearly, to see things as they are. She really believed that

> Earth reserves no blessing
> For the unblest of heaven;

and she had an almost Calvinistic sense of her own condemnation to unhappiness. That being so, she was suspicious of those opportunities of joy which did come to her, or at least resolute not to believe too implicitly in the good messages of the stars, which might be mere dreams, or of the earth, which was only certainly kind in preparing for her that often-thought-of grave. 'No coward soul is mine' is one of her true sayings; but it was with difficulty that she trusted even that message of life which she seemed to discover in death. She has to assure herself of it, again and again: 'Who once lives, never dies!' And that sense of personal identity which aches throughout all her poems is a sense, not of the delight, but of the pain and ineradicable sting of personal identity.

Her poems are all outcries, as her great novel, *Wuthering*

Heights, is one long outcry. A soul on the rack seems to make itself heard at moments, when suffering has grown too acute for silence. Every poem is as if torn from her. Even when she does not write seemingly in her own person, the subjects are such disguises as 'The Prisoner,' 'Honour's Martyr,' 'The Outcast Mother,' echoes of all the miseries and useless rebellions of the earth. She spells over the fading characters in dying faces, unflinchingly, with an austere curiosity; and looks[Pg 114] closely into the eyes of shame, not dreading what she may find there. She is always arguing with herself, and the answers are inflexible, the answers of a clear intellect which rebels but accepts defeat. Her doubt is itself an affirmation, her defiance would be an entreaty but for the 'quenchless will' of her pride. She faces every terror, and to her pained apprehension birth and death and life are alike terrible. Only Webster's dirge might have been said over her coffin.

> What my soul bore my soul alone
> Within itself may tell,

she says truthfully; but some of that long endurance of her life, in which exile, the body's weakness, and a sense of some 'divinest anguish' which clung about the world and all things living, had their share, she was able to put into ascetic and passionate verse. It is sad-coloured and desolate, but when gleams of sunlight or of starlight pierce the clouds that hang generally above it, a rare and stormy beauty comes into the bare outlines, quickening them with living splendour.

AN EXCERPT FROM
Figures of Several Centuries, 1906

CHARLOTTE BRONTË

***

BY ELBERT HUBBARD

"I was not surprised, when I went down into the hall, to see that a brilliant June morning had succeeded to the tempest of the night, and to feel through the open glass door the breathing of a fresh and fragrant breeze. Nature must be gladsome when I was so happy. A beggar woman and her little boy, pale, ragged objects both, were coming up the walk, and I ran down and gave them all the money I happened to have in my purse—some three or four shillings: good or bad they must partake of my jubilee. The rooks cawed and blither birds sung, but nothing was so merry or so musical as my own rejoicing heart"

—JANE EYRE

Rumor has it that there be Americans who are never happy unless passing for Englishmen. And I think I have discovered a like anomaly on the part of the sons of Ireland—a wish to pass for Frenchmen. On Continental hotel-registers the good, honest name of O'Brian often turns queer somersaults, and more than once in "The States" does the kingly prefix of O evolve itself into Van or De, which perhaps is quite proper, seeing they all mean the same thing. One cause of this tendency may lie in the fact that Saint Patrick was a native of France; although Saint Patrick may or may not have been chosen patron saint on account of his nationality. But the patron saint of Ireland being a Frenchman, what more natural, and therefore what more proper, than that the whole Emerald Isle should slant toward the people who love art and rabbit-stew! Anyway, from the proud patronymic of

151

Patricius to plain Pat is quite a drop, and my heart is with Paddy in his efforts to get back.

When Patrick Prunty of County Down, Ireland, shook off the shackles of environment, and the mud of the peat-bog, and went across to England, presenting himself at the gates of Saint John's College, Cambridge, asking for admittance, I am glad he handed in his name as Mr. P. Bronte, accent on the last syllable.

There is a gentle myth abroad that preachers are "called," while other men adopt a profession or get a job, but no Protestant Episcopal clergyman I have ever known, and I have known many, ever made any such claim. They take up the profession because it supplies honors and a "living." Then they can do good, too, and all men want to do good. So they hie them to a divinity school and are taught the mysteries of theological tierce and thrust; and interviewing a clerical tailor they are ready to accept the honors and partake of the living. After a careful study of the life of Patrick Bronte I can not find that his ambition extended beyond the desirable things I have named—that is to say, inclusively, honors and a living.

He was tall, athletic, dark, and surely a fellow of force and ambition to set his back on the old and boldly rap for admittance at the gates of Cambridge. He was a pretty good student, too, although a bit quarrelsome and sometimes mischievous—throwing his force into quite unnecessary ways, as Irishmen are apt to do. He fell in love, of course, and has not an Irishman in love been likened to Vesuvius in state of eruption? We know of at least one charming girl who refused to marry him, because he declined, unlike Othello, to tell the story of his life. And it was assumed that any man who would not tell who "his folks" were, was a rogue and a varlet and a vagrom at heart. And all the while Monsieur Bronte had nothing worse to conceal than that he was from County Down and his name Prunty. He wouldn't give in and tell the story of his life to slow music, and so the girl wept and then stormed, and finally Bronte stormed and went away, and the girl and her parents were sure that the Frenchman was a murderer escaping justice. Fortunate, aye, thrice fortunate is it for the world that neither Bronte nor the girl wavered even in the estimation of a hair.

Bronte got through school and came out with tuppence worth of honors. When thirty, we find him established as curate at the shabby little town of Hartshead, in Yorkshire. Little Miss Branwell, from Penzance, came up there on a visit to her uncle, and the Reverend Mr. Bronte at once fell violently in love with her dainty form and gentle ways. I say "violently," for that's the kind of man Bronte was. Darwin says, "The faculty of amativeness is not aroused except by the unfamiliar." Girls who go away visiting, wearing their best bib and tucker, find lovers without fail. One-third of all marriages in the United States occur in just this way: the bib and tucker being sprung on the young man as a surprise, dazzles and hypnotizes him into an avowal and an engagement.

And so they were married—were the Reverend Patrick Bronte and Miss Maria Branwell. He was big, bold and dictatorial; she was little, shy and sensitive. The babies came—one in less than a year, then a year apart. The dainty little woman had her troubles, we are sure of that. Her voice comes to us only as a plaintive echo. When she asked to have the bread passed, she always apologized. Once her aunt sent her a present of a pretty silk dress, for country clergymen's wives do not have many luxuries—don't you know that?—and Patrick Bronte cut the dress into strips before her eyes and then threw the pieces, and the little slippers to match, into the fireplace, to teach his wife humility. He used to practise with a pistol and shoot in the house to steady the lady's nerves, and occasionally he got plain drunk. A man like Bronte in a little town with a tired little wife, and with inferior people, is a despot. He busies himself with trifles, looks after foolish details, and the neighbors let him have his own way and his wife has to, and the result is that he becomes convinced in his own mind that he is the people and that wisdom will die with him.

And yet Bronte wrote some pretty good poetry, and had faculties that rightly developed might have made him an excellent man. He should have gone down to London (or up, because it is south) and there come into competition with men as strong as himself. Fate should have seized him by the hair and bumped his head against stone walls and cuffed him thoroughly, and kicked him into line, teaching him humility, then out of the scrimmage we might have gotten a really superior product.

Mrs. Bronte became a confirmed invalid. A man can not always badger a woman; God is good—she dies. Little Maria Branwell had been married eight years; when she passed out she left six children, "all of a size," a neighbor woman has written. Over her grave is a tablet erected by her husband informing the wayfarer that "she has gone to meet her Savior." At the bottom is this warning to all women: "Be ye also ready; for in such an hour as ye think not the Son of Man cometh."

Five of these motherless children were girls and one a boy.

As you stand there in that stone church at Haworth reading the inscription above Maria Branwell's grave, you can also read the death record of the babes she left. The mother died on September Fifteenth, Eighteen Hundred Twenty-one; her oldest daughter, Maria, on May Sixth, Eighteen Hundred Twenty-five; Elizabeth, June Fifteenth, Eighteen Hundred Twenty-five; Patrick Branwell, on September Twenty-fourth, Eighteen Hundred Forty-eight; Emily, December Nineteenth, Eighteen Hundred Forty-eight; Anne, May Twenty-eighth, Eighteen Hundred Forty-nine; and Charlotte, on March Thirty-first, Eighteen Hundred Fifty-five. Those whom the gods love die young: the Reverend Patrick Bronte lived to be eighty-five years old.

* * * * *

I got out of the train at Keighley, which you must pronounce "Keethley," and leaving my valise with the station-master started on foot for Haworth, four miles away.

Keighley is a manufacturing town where various old mansions have been turned into factories, and new factories have sprung up, square, spick-span, trimmed-stone buildings, with fire-escapes and red tanks on top.

One of these old mansions I saw had a fine copper roof that shone in the sun like a monster Lake Superior agate. It stands a bit back from the road, and on one great gatepost is a brass plate reading "Cardigan Hall," and on the other a sign, "No Admittance—Apply at the Office." So I applied at the office, which is evidently the ancient lodge, and asked if Mr. Cardigan was in. Four clerks perched on high stools, crouching over big ledgers, dropped their pens and turning on their spiral seats looked at me with staring eyes, and with mouths wide open. I repeated the question and one of the quartette, a wheezy little old man in spectacles and with whiskers on his neck, clambered down from his elevated position and ambled over near, walking around me, eying me curiously.

"Go wan wi' yer wurruk, ye idlers!" he suddenly commanded the others. And then he explained to me that Mr. Cardigan was not in, neither was Mr. Jackson. In fact, Mr. Cardigan had not been in for a hundred years—being dead. But if I wanted to look at goods I could be accommodated with bargains fully five per cent below Lunnon market. The little old man was in such serious earnest that I felt it would be a sin to continue a joke. I explained that I was only a tourist in search of the picturesque, and thereby did I drop ten points in the old man's estimation. But this did I learn, that Lord Cardigan has won deathless fame by attaching his name to a knit jacket, just as the name Jaeger will go clattering down the corridors of time attached to a "combination suit."

This splendid old mansion was once the ancestral home of a branch of the noble family of Cardigan. But things got somewhat shuffled, through too many hot suppers up to London (being south), and stacks of reds and stacks of blues were drawn in towards the dealer, and so the old mansion fell under the hammer of the auctioneer. What an all-powerful thing is an auctioneer's hammer! And now from the great parlors, and the library, and the "hall," and the guest-chambers echo the rattle of spinning-jennies and the dull booming of whirling pulleys. And above the song of whirring wheels came the songs of girls at their work—voices that alone might have been harsh and discordant, but blending with the monotone of the factory's roar were really melodious.

"We cawn't keep the nasty things from singin'," said the old man apologetically.

"Why should you?" I asked.

"Huh, mon! but they sing sacred songs, and chaunts, and a' that, and say all together from twenty rooms, a hundred times a day, 'Aws ut wuz in th' beginnin',' uz now awn ever shawl be, worl' wi'out end, Aamen.' It's not right. I've told Mr. Jackson. Listen now, didn't I tell ye?"

"Then you are a Churchman?"

And the old man wiped his glasses and told me that he was a Churchman, although an unworthy one, and had been for fifty-four years, come Michaelmas. Yes, he had always lived here, was born only across the beck away—his father was gamekeeper for Lord Cardigan, and afterwards agent. He had been to Haworth many times, although not for ten years. He knew the Reverend Patrick Bronte well, for the Incumbent from Haworth used to preach at Keighley once a year, and sometimes twice. Bronte was a fine man, with a splendid voice for intoning, and very strict about keeping out all heresies and such. He had a lot of trouble, had Bronte: his wife died and left him with eight or ten children, all smart, but rather wild. They gave him a lot of bother, especially the boy. One of the girls married Mr. Bronte's curate, Mr. Nicholls, a very decent kind of man who comes to Keighley once a year, and always comes to the factory to ask how things are going.

Yes, Mr. Nicholls' first wife died years and years ago. She used to write things—novels; but no one should read novels; novels are stories that are not so—things that never happened; they tell of folks that never was.

Having no argument to present in way of rebuttal, I shook

hands with the old man and started away. He walked with me to the road to put me on the right way to Haworth.

Looking back as I reached the corner, I saw four "clarks" watching me intently from the office windows, and above the roar and jangle of machinery was borne on the summer breeze the sound of sacred song—shrill feminine voices:

"Aws ut wuz in th' beginnin', uz now awn ever shawl be, worl' wi'out end—Aamen!"

* * * * *

As one moves out of Keighley the country becomes stony; the trees are left behind, and there rises on all sides billow on billow of purple heather. The way is rough as the Pilgrim's Progress road to Paradise. These hillside moors are filled with springs that high up form rills, then brooks, then cascades or "becks," and along the Haworth road, wherever one of these hurrying, scurrying, dancing becks crosses the highway, there is a factory devoted to keeping alive the name of Cardigan. Next to the factory is a "pub.," and publics and factories checker themselves all along the route. Mixed in with these are long rows of tenement-houses well built of stone, with slate roofs, but with a grimy air of desolation about them that surely drives their occupants to drink. To have a home a man must build it himself. Forty houses in a row, all alike, are not homes at all.

I believe an observant man once wrote of the hand being subdued to what it works in. The man who wrote that surely never tramped along the Haworth road as the bell rang for twelve o'clock. From out the factories poured a motley mob of men, women and children, not only with hands dyed, but with clothing, faces and heads as well. Girls with bright-green hair, and lemon-colored faces, leered and jeered at me as they hastened pellmell with hats askew, and stockings down, and dragging shawls, for home or public-house. Red and maroon children ran, and bright-scarlet men smoked stolidly, taking their time with genuine grim Yorkshire sullen sourness.

"How far is it to Haworth?" I asked one such specimen.

"Ef ye pay th' siller for a double pot a' 'arf and 'arf. Hi might tell ye"; and he jerked his thumb over his shoulder toward a ginshop near by.

"Very well," said I; "I'll buy you a double pot of 'arf and 'arf, this time."

The man seemed a bit surprised, but no smile came over his spattered rainbow face as he led the way into the drink-shop. The place was crowded with men and women scrambling for penny sandwiches and drinks fermented and spirituous. Some of these women had babies at their breasts, the babies being brought by appointment by older children who stayed at home while the mothers worked. And as the mothers gulped their Triple XXX, and swallowed hunks of black bread, the little innocents dined. The mothers were rather kindly disposed, though, and occasionally allowed the youngsters to take sips out of their foaming glasses, or at least to drain them. Suddenly a woman with purple hair spied me and called in falsetto:

"Ah, Sawndy McClure has caught a gen'l'mon. Why didn't I see 'im fust an' 'arve 'im fer a pet?"

There was a guffaw at my expense and 'arf and 'arf as well, for all the party, or else quarrel. As it was, my stout stick probably saved me from the "personal touch." I stayed until the factory-bells rang, and out my new-found friends scurried for fear of being the fatal five minutes late and getting locked out. Some of them shook my hand as they went, and others pounded me on the back for luck, and several of the girls got my tag and shouted, "You're it!"

I used to think that Yorkshire folks were hopelessly dull and sublimely stupid, quarrelsome withal and pigheaded to the thirty-second degree; but I have partially come to the conclusion that their glum ways often conceal a peculiar kind of grim humor, and beneath the tough husk is considerable good nature.

The absence of large trees makes it possible to see the village of Haworth several miles away. It seems to cling to the stony hillside as if it feared being blown into space. There is a hurrying, rushing rill here, too, that turns a little woolen-mill. Then there is a "Black Bull" tavern, with a stable-yard at the side and rows of houses on the one street, all very straight up and down. One misses the climbing roses of the ideal merry England, and the soft turf and spreading yews and the flowering hedgerows where throstles and linnets play hide-and-seek the livelong day. It is all cold gray stone, lichen-covered, and the houses do not invite you to enter, and the gardens bid no welcome, and only the great purple wastes of moorland greet you as a friend and brother.

Outside the Black Bull sits a solitary hostler, who feels it would be a weakness to show any good humor. So he bottles his curiosity and scowls from under red, bushy eyebrows.

Turning off the main street is a narrow road leading to the church—square and gray and cold. Next to it is the parsonage, built of the same material, and beyond is the crowded city of the dead.

I plied the knocker at the parsonage door and asked for the rector. He was away at Kendal to attend a funeral, but his wife was at home—a pleasant, matronly woman of near sixty, with smooth, white hair. She came to the door knitting furiously, but from her regulation smile I saw that visitors were not uncommon.

"You want to see the home of the Brontes? That's right, come right in. This was the study of the Reverend Patrick Bronte, Incumbent of this Parish for fifty years."

She sang her little song and knitted and shifted the needles and measured the foot, for the stocking was nearly done. It was a blue stocking (although she wasn't) with a white toe; and all the time she led me from room to room telling me about the Brontes—how there were the father, mother and six children. They all came together. The mother died shortly, and then two of the little girls died. That left three girls and Branwell the boy. He was petted and made too much of by his father and everybody. He was the one that always was going to do great things. He made the girls wait on him and cuffed them if they didn't, and if they did, and all the time told of the things he was going to do. But he never did them, for he spent most of his time at the taverns. After a while he died—died of the tremens.

The three Bronte girls, Emily, Charlotte and Annie, wrote a novel apiece, and never showed them to their father or to any one. They called 'emselves Currer, Ellis and Acton Bell, and their novels were the greatest ever written—they wrote them 'emselves with no man to help. Their father was awful mad about it, but when the money began to come in he felt better. Emily died when she was twenty-seven. She was the brightest of them all; then Annie died, and only Charlotte and the old man were left. Charlotte married her father's curate, but old Mr. Bronte wouldn't go to the wedding: he went to the Black Bull instead. Miss Wooler gave the bride away—some one had to give her away, you know. The bride was thirty-eight. She died in less them a year, and old Mr. Bronte and Charlotte's husband lived here alone together.

This was Charlotte's room; this is the desk where she wrote "Jane Eyre"—leastwise they say it is. This is the chair she sat in, and under that framed glass are several sheets of her manuscript. The writing is almost too small to read; and so fine and yet so perfect and neat! She was a wonderful tidy body, very small and delicate and gentle, yet with a good deal of her father's energy.

Here are letters she wrote: you can look at them if you choose. This footstool she made and covered herself. It is filled with heather-blossoms—just as she left it. Those books were hers, too—many of them given to her by great authors. See, there is Thackeray's name written by himself, and a letter from him pasted inside the front cover. He was a big man they say, but he wrote very small, and Charlotte wrote just like him, only better, and now there are hundreds of folks write like 'em both. Then here's a book with Miss Martineau's name, and another from Robert Browning—do you know who he was?

Yes, the church is always open. Go in and stay as long as you choose; at the door is a poorbox and if you wish to put something in you can do so—a sixpence most visitors put in, or a shilling if you insist upon it. You know we are not a rich parish—the wool all goes to Manchester now, and the factory-hands are on half-pay and times are scarce. You will come again some time, come when the heather is in bloom, won't you? That's right. Oh, stay! the boxwood there in the garden was planted by Charlotte's own hands—perhaps you would like a sprig of it—there, I thought you would!

* * * * *

All who write concerning the Brontes dwell on the sadness and the tragedy of their lives. They picture Charlotte's earth-journey as one devoid of happiness, lacking all that sweetens and makes for satisfaction. They forget that she wrote "Jane Eyre," and that no person utterly miserable ever did a great work; and I assume that they know not of the wild, splendid, intoxicating joy that follows a performance well done. To be sure, "Jane Eyre" is a tragedy, but the author of a tragedy must be greater than the plot—greater than his puppets. He is their creator, and his life runs through and pervades theirs, just as the life of our Creator flows through us. In Him we live and move and have our being. And I submit that the writer of a tragedy is not cast down or undone at the time he pictures his heroic situations and conjures forth his strutting spirits. When the play ends and the curtain falls on the fifth act, there is still one man alive, and that is the author. He may be gorged with crime and surfeited with blood, but there is a surging exultation in his veins as he views the ruin that his brain has wrought.

Charlotte loved the great stretch of purple moors, hill on hill fading away into eternal mist. And the wild winds that sighed and moaned at casements or raged in sullen wrath, tugging at the roof, were her friends. She loved them all, and thought of them as visiting spirits. They were her properties, and no writer who ever lived has made such splendid use of winds and storm-clouds and driving rain as did Charlotte Bronte. People who point to the chasing, angry clouds and the swish of dripping rosebushes blown against the cottage-windows as proof of Charlotte Bronte's chronic depression know not the eager joy of a storm walk. And I am sure they never did as one I know did last night: saddle a horse at ten o'clock and gallop away into the darkness; splash, splash in the sighing, moaning, bellowing, driving November rain. There's joy for you! ye who toast your feet on the fender and cultivate sick headache around the base-burner—there's a life that ye never guess!

But Charlotte knew the clouds by night and the swift-sailing moon that gave just one peep out and disappeared. She knew the rifts where the stars shone through, and out alone in the breeze that blew away her cares she lifted her voice in thankfulness for the joy of mixing with the elements, and that her spirit was one with the boisterous winds of heaven.

People who live in beautiful, quiet valleys, where roses bloom all the year through, are not necessarily happy.

Southern California—the Garden of Eden of the world— evolves just as many cases per capita of melancholia as bleak, barren Maine. Wild, rocky, forbidding Scotland has produced more genius to the acre than beautiful England: and I have found that sailor Jack, facing the North Atlantic winter storms, year after year, is a deal jollier companion than the Florida cracker whose chief adversary is the mosquito.

Charlotte Bronte wrote three great books: "Jane Eyre," "Shirley" and "Villette." From the lonely, bleak parsonage on that stony hillside she sent forth her swaying filament of thought and lassoed the world. She lived to know that she had won. Money came to her, all she needed, honors, friends and lavish praise. She was the foremost woman author of her day. Her name was on every tongue. She had met the world in fair fight; without patrons, paid advocates, or influential friends she made her way to the very front. Her genius was acknowledged. She accomplished all that she set out to do and more—far more. The great, the learned, the titled, the proud—all those who reverence the tender heart and far-reaching mind—acknowledged her as queen.

So why prate of her sorrows! Did she not work them up into art? Why weep over her troubles when these were the weapons with which she won? Why sit in sackcloth on account of her early death, when it is appointed unto all men once to die, and with her the grave was swallowed up in victory?

AN EXCERPT FROM
Little Journeys to the
Homes of Famous Women, 1916

"JANE EYRE"
AND
"WUTHERING HEIGHTS"

BY VIRGINIA WOOLF

Of the hundred years that have passed since Charlotte Brontë was born, she, the centre now of so much legend, devotion, and literature, lived but thirty-nine. It is strange to reflect how different those legends might have been had her life reached the ordinary human span. She might have become, like some of her famous contemporaries, a figure familiarly met with in London and elsewhere, the subject of pictures and anecdotes innumerable, the writer of many novels, of memoirs possibly, removed from us well within the memory of the middle-aged in all the splendour of established fame. She might have been wealthy, she might have been prosperous. But it is not so. When we think of her we have to imagine some one who had no lot in our modern world; we have to cast our minds back to the 'fifties of the last century, to a remote parsonage upon the wild Yorkshire moors. In that parsonage, and on those moors, unhappy and lonely, in her poverty and her exaltation, she remains for ever.

These circumstances, as they affected her character, may have left their traces on her work. A novelist, we reflect, is bound to build up his structure with much very perishable material which begins by lending it reality and ends by cumbering it with rubbish. As we open Jane Eyre once more we cannot stifle the suspicion that we shall find her world of imagination as antiquated, mid-Victorian, and out of date as the parsonage on the moor, a place only to be visited by the curious, only preserved by the pious. So we open Jane Eyre; and in two pages every doubt is swept clean from our minds.

Folds of scarlet drapery shut in my view to the right hand; to the left were the clear panes of glass, protecting, but not separating me from the drear November day. At intervals, while turning over the leaves of my book, I studied the aspect of that winter afternoon. Afar, it offered a pale blank of mist and cloud; near, a scene of wet lawn and storm-beat shrub, with ceaseless rain sweeping away wildly before a long and lamentable blast.

There is nothing there more perishable than the moor itself, or more subject to the sway of fashion than the "long and lamentable blast". Nor is this exhilaration short-lived. It rushes us through the entire volume, without giving us time to think, without letting us lift our eyes from the page. So intense is our absorption that if some one moves in the room the movement seems to take place not there but up in Yorkshire. The writer has us by the hand, forces us along her road, makes us see what she sees, never leaves us for a moment or allows us to forget her. At the end we are steeped through and through with the genius, the vehemence, the indignation of Charlotte Brontë. Remarkable faces, figures of strong outline and gnarled feature have flashed upon us in passing; but it is through her eyes that we have seen them. Once she is gone, we seek for them in vain. Think of Rochester and we have to think of Jane Eyre. Think of the moor, and again there is Jane Eyre. Think of the drawing-room, even, those "white carpets on which seemed laid brilliant garlands of flowers", that "pale Parian mantelpiece" with its Bohemia glass of "ruby red" and the "general blending of snow and fire"— what is all that except Jane Eyre?

Charlotte and Emily Brontë had much the same sense of colour. " . . . we saw — ah! it was beautiful — a splendid place carpeted with crimson, and crimson-covered chairs and tables, and a pure white ceiling bordered by gold, a shower of glass drops hanging in silver chains from the centre, and shimmering with little soft tapers" (Wuthering Heights). "Yet it was merely a very pretty drawing-room, and within it a boudoir, both spread with white carpets, on which seemed laid brilliant garlands of flowers; both ceiled with snowy mouldings of white grapes and vine leaves, beneath which glowed in rich contrast crimson couches and ottomans; while the ornaments on the pale Parian mantelpiece were of sparkling Bohemia glass, ruby red; and between the windows large mirrors repeated the general blending of snow and fire" (Jane Eyre).

The drawbacks of being Jane Eyre are not far to seek. Always to be a governess and always to be in love is a serious limitation in a world which is full, after all, of people who are neither one nor the other. The characters of a Jane Austen or of a Tolstoi have a million facets compared with these. They live and are complex by means of their effect upon many different people who serve to mirror them in the round. They move hither and thither whether their creators watch them or not, and the world in which they live seems to us an independent world which we can visit, now that they have created it, by ourselves. Thomas Hardy is more akin to Charlotte Brontë in the power of his personality and the narrowness of his vision. But the differences are vast. As we read Jude the Obscure we are not rushed to a finish; we brood and ponder and drift away from the text in plethoric trains of thought which build up round the characters an atmosphere of question and suggestion of which they are themselves, as often as not, unconscious. Simple peasants as they are, we are forced to confront them with destinies and questionings of the hugest import, so that often it seems as if the most important characters in a Hardy novel are those which have no names. Of this power, of this speculative curiosity, Charlotte Brontë has no trace. She does not attempt to solve the problems of human life; she is even unaware that such problems exist; all her force, and it is the more tremendous for being constricted, goes into the assertion, "I love", "I hate", "I suffer".

For the self-centred and self-limited writers have a power denied the more catholic and broad-minded. Their impressions are close packed and strongly stamped between their narrow walls. Nothing issues from their minds which has not been marked with their own impress. They learn little from other writers, and what they adopt they cannot assimilate. Both Hardy and Charlotte Brontë appear to have founded their styles upon a stiff and decorous journalism. The staple of their prose is awkward and unyielding. But both with labour and the most obstinate integrity, by thinking every thought until it has subdued words to itself, have forged for themselves a prose which takes the mould of their minds entire; which has, into the bargain, a beauty, a power, a swiftness of its own. Charlotte Brontë, at least, owed nothing to the reading of many books. She never learnt the smoothness of the professional writer, or acquired his ability to stuff and sway his language as he chooses. "I could never rest in communication with strong, discreet, and refined minds, whether male or female", she writes, as any leader-writer in a provincial journal might have written; but gathering fire and speed goes on in her own authentic voice "till I had passed the outworks of conventional reserve and crossed the threshold of confidence, and won a place by their hearts' very hearthstone". It is there that she takes her seat; it is the red and fitful glow of the heart's fire which illumines her page. In other words, we read Charlotte Brontë not for exquisite observation of character — her characters are vigorous and elementary; not for comedy — hers is grim and crude; not for a philosophic view of life — hers is that of a country parson's daughter; but for her poetry. Probably that is so with all writers who have, as she has, an overpowering personality, so that, as we say in real life, they have only to open the door to make themselves felt. There is in them some untamed ferocity perpetually at war with the accepted order of things which makes them desire to create instantly rather than to observe patiently. This very ardour, rejecting half shades and other minor impediments, wings its way past the daily conduct of ordinary people and allies itself with their more inarticulate passions. It makes them poets, or, if they choose to write in prose, intolerant of its restrictions. Hence it is that both Emily and Charlotte are always invoking the help of nature. They both feel the need of some more powerful symbol of the vast and slumbering passions in human nature than words or actions can convey. It is with a description of a storm that Charlotte ends her finest novel Villette. "The skies hang full and dark — a wrack sails from the west; the clouds cast themselves into strange forms." So she calls in nature to describe a state of mind which could not otherwise be expressed. But neither of the sisters observed nature accurately as Dorothy Wordsworth observed it, or painted it minutely as Tennyson painted it. They seized those aspects of the earth which were most akin to what they themselves felt or imputed to their characters, and so their storms, their moors, their lovely spaces of summer weather are not ornaments applied to decorate a dull page or display the writer's powers of observation — they carry on the emotion and light up the meaning of the book.

The meaning of a book, which lies so often apart from what happens and what is said and consists rather in some connection which things in themselves different have had for the writer, is necessarily hard to grasp. Especially this is so when, like the Brontës, the writer is poetic, and his meaning inseparable from his language, and itself rather a mood than a particular observation. Wuthering Heights is a more difficult book to understand than Jane Eyre, because Emily was a greater poet than Charlotte. When Charlotte wrote she said with eloquence and splendour and passion "I love", "I hate", "I suffer". Her experience, though more intense, is on a level with our own. But there is no "I" in Wuthering Heights. There are no governesses. There are no employers. There is love, but it is not the love of men and women. Emily was inspired by some more general conception. The impulse which urged her to create was not her own suffering or her own injuries. She looked out upon a world cleft into gigantic disorder and felt within her the power to unite it in a book. That gigantic ambition is to be felt throughout the novel — a struggle, half thwarted but of superb conviction, to say something through the mouths of her characters which is not merely "I love" or "I hate", but "we, the whole human race" and "you, the eternal powers . . . " the sentence remains unfinished. It is not strange that it should be so; rather it is astonishing that she can make us feel what she had it in her to say at all. It surges up in the half-articulate words of Catherine Earnshaw, "If all else perished and HE remained, I should still continue to be; and if all else remained and he were annihilated, the universe would turn to a mighty stranger; I should not seem part of it". It breaks out again in the presence of the dead. "I see a repose that neither earth nor hell can break, and I feel an assurance of the endless and shadowless hereafter — the eternity they have entered — where life is boundless in its duration, and love in its sympathy and joy in its fulness." It is this suggestion of power underlying the apparitions of human nature and lifting them up into the presence of greatness that gives the book its huge stature among other novels. But it was not enough for Emily Brontë to write a few lyrics, to utter a cry, to express a creed. In her poems she did this once and for all, and her poems will perhaps outlast her novel. But she was novelist as well as poet. She must take upon herself a more laborious and a more ungrateful task. She must face the fact of other existences, grapple with the mechanism of external things, build up, in recognisable shape, farms and houses and report the speeches of men and women who existed independently of herself. And so we reach these summits of emotion not by rant or rhapsody but by hearing a girl sing old songs to herself as she rocks in the branches of a tree; by watching the moor sheep crop the turf; by listening to the soft wind breathing through the grass. The life at the farm with all its absurdities and its improbability is laid open to us. We are given every opportunity of comparing Wuthering Heights with a real farm and Heathcliff with a real man. How, we are allowed to ask, can there be truth or insight or the finer shades of emotion in men and women who so little resemble what we have seen ourselves? But even as we ask it we see in Heathcliff the brother that a sister of genius might have seen; he is impossible we say, but nevertheless no boy in literature has a more vivid existence than his. So it is with the two Catherines; never could women feel as they do or act in their manner, we say. All the same, they are the most lovable women in English fiction. It is as if she could tear up all that we know human beings by, and fill these unrecognisable transparences with such a gust of life that they transcend reality. Hers, then, is the rarest of all powers. She could free life from its dependence on facts; with a few touches indicate the spirit of a face so that it needs no body; by speaking of the moor make the wind blow and the thunder roar.

AN EXCERPT FROM
The Common Reader, 1916

EMILY BRONTË

BY JOHN COWPER POWYS

The name of Emily Brontë—why does it produce in one's mind so strange and startling a feeling, unlike that produced by any other famous writer?

It is not easy to answer such a question. Certain great souls seem to gather to themselves, as their work accumulates its destined momentum in its voyage down the years, a power of arousing our imagination to issues that seem larger than those which can naturally be explained as proceeding inevitably from their tangible work.

Our imagination is roused and our deepest soul stirred by the mention of such names without any palpable accompaniment of logical analysis, without any well-weighed or rational justification.

Such names touch some response in us which goes deeper than our critical faculties, however desperately they may struggle. Instinct takes the place of reason; and our soul, as if answering the appeal of some translunar chord of subliminal music, vibrates in response to a mood that baffles all analysis.

We all know the work of Emily's sister Charlotte; we know it and can return to it at will, fathoming easily and at leisure the fine qualities of it and its impassioned and romantic effect upon us.

But though we may have read over and over again that one amazing story—"Wuthering Heights"—and that handful of unforgettable poems which are all that Emily Brontë has bequeathed to the world, which of us can say that the full significance of these things has been ransacked and combed out by our conscious reason; which of us can say that we understand to the full all the mysterious stir and ferment, all the far-reaching and magical reactions, which such things have produced within us?

Who can put into words the secret of this extraordinary girl? Who can define, in the suave and plausible language of academic culture, the flitting shadows thrown from deep to deep in the unfathomable genius of her vision?

Perhaps not since Sappho has there been such a person. Certainly she makes the ghosts of de Staël and Georges Sand, of Eliot and Mrs. Browning, look singularly homely and sentimental.

I am inclined to think that the huge mystery of Emily Brontë's power lies in the fact that she expresses in her work—just as the Lesbian, did—the very soul of womanhood. It is not an easy thing to achieve, this. Women writers, clever and lively and subtle, abound in our time, as they have abounded in times past; but for some inscrutable reason they lack the demonic energy, the occult spiritual force, the instinctive fire, wherewith to give expression to the ultimate mystery of their own sex.

I am inclined to think that, of all poets, Walt Whitman is the only one who has drawn his reckless and chaotic inspiration straight from the uttermost spiritual depths of the sex-instincts of the male animal; and Emily Brontë has done for her sex what Walt Whitman did for his.

It is a strange and startling commentary upon the real significance of our sexual impulses that, when it comes to the final issue, it is not the beautiful ruffianism of a Byron, full of normal sex-instinct though that may be, or the eloquent sentiment of a Georges Sand, penetrated with passionate sensuality as that is, which really touch the indefinable secret. Emily Brontë, like Walt Whitman, sweeps us, by sheer force of inspired genius, into a realm where the mere *animalism* of sexuality, its voluptuousness, its lust, its lechery, are absolutely merged, lost, forgotten; fused by that burning flame of spiritual passion into something which is beyond all earthly desire.

Emily Brontë—and this is indicative of the difference between woman and man—goes even further than Walt Whitman in the spiritualising of this flame. In Whitman there is, as we all know, a vast mass of work, wherein, true and magical though it is, the earthly and bodily elements of the great passion are given enormous emphasis. It is only at rare moments—as happens with ordinary men in the normal experience of the world—that he is swept away beyond the reach of lust and voluptuousness. But Emily Brontë seems to dwell by natural predilection upon these high summits and in these unsounded depths. The flame of the passion in her burns at such quivering vibrant pressure that the fuel of it—the debris and rubble of our earth-instincts— is entirely absorbed and devoured. In her work the fire of life licks up, with its consuming tongue, every vestige of materiality in the thing upon which it feeds, and the lofty tremulous spires of its radiant burning ascend into the illimitable void.

It is of extraordinary interest, as a mere psychological phenomenon, to note the fact that when the passion of sex is driven forward by the flame of its conquering impulse beyond a certain point it becomes itself transmuted and loses the earthy texture of its original character.

Sex-passion when carried to a certain pitch of intensity loses its sexuality. It becomes pure flame; immaterial, unearthly, and with no sensual dross left in it.

It may even be said, by an enormous paradox, to become sexless. And this is precisely what one feels about the work of Emily Brontë. Sex-passion in her has been driven so far that it has come round "full circle" and has become sexless passion. It has become passion disembodied, passion absolute, passion divested of all human weakness.

The "muddy vesture of decay" which "grossly closes in" our diviner principle has been burnt up and absorbed. It has been reduced to nothing; and in its place quivers up to heaven the clear white flame of the secret fountain of life.

But there is more in the matter than that. Emily Brontë's genius, by its abandonment to the passion of which I have been speaking, does not only burn up and destroy all the elements of clay in what, so to speak, is above the earth and on its surface; but it also, burning downwards, destroys and annihilates all dubious and obscure materials which surround the original and primordial human will. Round and about this lonely and inalienable will it makes a scorched and blackened plain of ashes and cinders. Ambiguous feelings are turned to ashes there; and so are doubts, hesitations, timidities, trepidations, cowardices. The aboriginal will of man, of the unconquerable individual, stands alone there in the twilight, under the grey desolate rain of the outer spaces. Four-square it stands, upon adamantine foundations, and nothing in heaven or earth is able to shake it or disquiet it.

It is this isolation, in desolate and forlorn integrity, of the individual human will, which is the deepest element in Emily Brontë's genius. Upon this all depends, and to this all returns. Between the will and the spirit deep and strange nuptials are celebrated; and from the immortality of the spirit a certain breath of life passes over into the mortality of the will, drawing it up into the celestial and invisible region which is beyond chance and change.

From this abysmal fusion of the "creator spiritus" with the human will rises that adamantine courage with which Emily Brontë was able to face the jagged edges of that crushing wheel of destiny which the malign powers of nature drive remorselessly over our poor flesh and blood. The uttermost spirit of the universe became in this manner *her* spirit, and the integral identity of the soul within her breast hardened into an undying resistance to all that would undermine it.

Thus she was able to endure tragedy upon tragedy without flinching. Thus she was able to assert herself against the power of pain as one wrestling invincibly with an exhausted giant.

Calamity after calamity fell upon her house, and the stark desolation of those melancholy Yorkshire hills became a suitable and congruous background for the loneliness of her strange life; but against all the pain which came upon her, against all the aching pangs of remorseless fate, this indomitable girl held grimly to her supreme vision.

No poet, no novelist who has ever lived has been so profoundly affected by the conditions of his life as was this invincible woman. But the conditions of her life—the scenery of sombre terror which surrounded her—only touched and affected the outward colour and rhythm of her unique style. In her deepest soul, in the courage of her tremendous vision, she possessed something that was not bounded by Yorkshire hills, or any other hills; something that was inhuman, eternal and universal, something that was outside the power of both time and space.

By that singular and forlorn scenery—the scenery of the Yorkshire moors round about her home—she was, however, in the more flexible portion of her curious nature inveterately influenced. She does not precisely describe this scenery—not at any rate at any length—either in her poems or in "Wuthering Heights"; but it sank so deeply into her that whatever she wrote was affected by it and bears its desolate and imaginative imprint.

It is impossible to read Emily Brontë anywhere without being transported to those Yorkshire moors. One smells the smell of burning furze, one tastes the resinous breath of pine-trees, one feels beneath one's feet the tough fibrous stalks of the ling and the resistant stems and crumpled leaves of the bracken.

Dark against that pallid greenish light of a dead sunset, which is more than anything else characteristic of those unharvested fells, one can perceive always, as one reads her, the sombre form of some gigantic Scotch-fir stretching out its arms across the sky; while a flight of rooks, like enormous black leaves drifting on the wind, sail away into the sunset at our approach.

One is conscious, as one reads her, of lonely marsh-pools turning empty faces towards a grey heaven, while drop by drop upon their murky waters the autumn rain falls, sadly, wearily, without aim or purpose.

And most of all is one made aware of the terrible desolation—desolation only rendered more desolate by the presence of humanity—of those half-ruined farm-houses, approached by windy paths or deep-cut lanes, which seem to rise, like huge fungoid things, here and there over that sad land.

It is difficult to conceive they have not sprung—these dwellings of these Earnshaws and Lintons—actually out of the very soil, in slow organic growth leading to slow organic decay. One cannot conceive the human hands which *built* them; any more than one can conceive the human hands which planted those sombre hedges which have now become so completely part of the scenery that one thinks of them as quite as aboriginal to the place as the pine-trees or the gorse-bushes.

Of all shapes of all trees I think the shape of an old and twisted thorn-tree harmonises best with one's impression of the "milieu" of Emily Brontë's single tragic story; a thorn-tree distorted by the wind blowing from one particular quarter, and with its trunk blackened and hollowed; and in the hollow of it a little pool of rain-water and a few dead soaked leaves.

The extraordinary thing is that she can produce these impressions incidentally, and, as it were, unconsciously. They are so blent with her spirit, these things, that they convey themselves to one's mind indirectly and through a medium far more subtle than any eloquent description.

I cannot think of Emily Brontë's work without thinking of a certain tree I once saw against a pallid sky. A long way from Yorkshire it was where I saw this tree, and there were no limestone boulders scattered at its feet; but something in the impression it produced upon me—an impression I shall not lightly forget—weaves itself strangely in with all I feel about her, so that the peculiar look of wintry boughs, sad and silent against a fading west, accompanied by that natural human longing of people who are tired to be safely buried under the friendly earth and "free among the dead," has come to be most indelibly and deeply associated with her tragic figure.

Those who know those Yorkshire moors know the mysterious way in which the quiet country lanes suddenly emerge upon wide and desolate expanses; know how they lead us on, past ruined factories and deserted quarries, up the barren slopes of forlorn hills; know how, as one sees in front of one the long white road vanishing over the hill-top and losing itself in the grey sky, there comes across one's mind a strange, sad, exquisite feeling unlike any other feeling in the world; and we who love Emily Brontë know that this is the feeling, the mood, the atmosphere of the soul, into which her writings throw us.

The power of her great single story, "Wuthering Heights," is in a primary sense the power of romance, and none can care for this book for whom romance means nothing.

What is romance? I think it is the instinctive recognition of a certain poetic glamour which an especial kind of grouping of persons and things—of persons and things seen under a particular light—is able to produce. It does not always accompany the expression of passionate emotion or the narration of thrilling incidents. These may arrest and entertain us when there is no romance, in my sense at any rate of that great word, overshadowing the picture.

I think this quality of romance can only be evoked when the background of the story is heavily laden with old, rich, dim, pathetic, human associations. I think it can only emerge when there is an implication of thickly mingled traditions, full of sombre and terrible and beautiful suggestiveness, stimulating to the imagination like a draught of heavy red wine. I think there must be, in a story of which the flavour has the true romantic magic, something darkly and inexplicably fatal. I think it is necessary that one should hear the rush of the flight of the Valkyries and the wailing upon the wind of the voices of the Eumenides.

Fate—in such a story—must assume a half-human, half-personal shape, and must brood, obscurely and sombrely, over the incidents and the characters.

The characters themselves must be swayed and dominated by Fate; and not only by Fate. They must be penetrated through and through by the scenery which surrounds them and by the traditions, old and dark and superstitious and malign, of some particular spot upon the earth's surface.

The scenery which is the background of a tale which has the true romantic quality must gather itself together and concentrate itself in some kind of symbolic unity; and this symbolic unity— wherein the various elements of grandeur and mystery are merged—must present itself as something almost personal and as a dynamic "motif" in the development of the plot.

There can be no romance without some sort of appeal to that long-inherited and atavistic feeling in ordinary human hearts which is responsive to the spell and influence of old, unhappy, lovely, ancient things; things faded and falling, but with the mellowness of the centuries upon their faces.

In other words, nothing can be romantic which is *new*. Romance implies, above everything else, a long association with the human feelings of many generations. It implies an appeal to that background of our minds which is stirred to reciprocity by suggestions dealing with those old, dark, mysterious memories which belong, not so much to us as individuals, as to us as links in a great chain.

There are certain emotions in all of us which go much further and deeper than our mere personal feelings. Such are the emotions roused in us by contact with the mysterious forces of life and death and birth and the movements of the seasons; with the rising and setting of the sun, and the primordial labour of tilling the earth and gathering in the harvest. These things have been so long associated with our human hopes and fears, with the nerves and fibres of our inmost being, that any powerful presentment of them brings to the surface the accumulated feelings of hundreds of centuries.

New problems, new adventures, new social groupings, new philosophical catchwords, may all have their vivid and exciting interest. They cannot carry with them that sad, sweet breath of planetary romance which touches what might be called the "imagination of the race" in individual men and women.

"Wuthering Heights" is a great book, not only because of the intensity of the passions in it, but because these passions are penetrated so profoundly with the long, bitter, tragic, human associations of persons who have lived for generations upon the same spot and have behind them the weight of the burden of the sorrows of the dead.

It is a great book because the romance of it emerges into undisturbed amplitude of space, and asserts itself in large, grand, primitive forms unfretted by teasing irrelevancies.

The genius of a romantic novelist—indeed, the genius of all writers primarily concerned with the mystery of human character—consists in letting the basic differences between man and man, between man and woman, rise up, unimpeded by frivolous detail, from the fathomless depths of life itself.

The solitude in which Emily Brontë lived, and the austere simplicity of her granite-moulded character, made it possible for her to envisage life in larger, simpler, less blurred outlines than most of us are able to do. Thus her art has something of that mysterious and awe-inspiring simplicity that characterises the work of Michelangelo or William Blake.

No one who has ever read "Wuthering Heights" can forget the place and the time when he read it. As I write its name now, every reader of this page will recall, with a sudden heavy sigh at the passing of youth, the moment when the sweet tragic power of its deadly genius first took him by the throat.

For me the shadow of an old bowed acacia-tree, held together by iron bands, was over the history of Heathcliff; but the forms and shapes of that mad drama gathered to themselves the lineaments of all my wildest dreams.

I can well remember, too, how on a certain long straight

road between Heathfield and Burwash, the eastern district of Sussex, my companion—the last of our English theologians—turned suddenly from his exposition of St. Thomas, and began quoting, as the white dust rose round us at the passing of a flock of sheep, the "vain are the thousand creeds—unutterably vain!" of that grand and absolute defiance, that last challenge of the unconquerable soul, which ends with the sublime cry to the eternal spark of godhead in us all—

> "Thou, thou art being and breath;
> And what thou art can never be destroyed!"

The art of Emily Brontë—if it can be called art, this spontaneous projection, in a shape rugged and savage, torn with the storms of fate, of her inmost identity—can be appreciated best if we realise with what skill we are plunged into the dark stream of the destiny of these people through the mediatory intervention of a comparative stranger. By this method, and also by the crafty manner in which she makes the old devoted servant of the house of Earnshaw utter a sort of Sophoclean commentary upon the events which take place, we are permitted to feel the magnitude of the thing in true relief and perspective.

By these devices we have borne in upon us, as in no other way could be done, the convincing sense which we require, to give weight and mass to the story, of the real continuity of life in those savage places.

By this method of narration we have the illusion of being suddenly initiated into a stream of events which are not merely imaginary. We have the illusion that these Earnshaws and Lintons are really, actually, palpably, undeniably, living—living somewhere, in their terrible isolation, as they have always lived—and that it is only by some lucky chance of casual discovery that we have been plunged into the mystery of their days.

One cannot help feeling aware, as we follow the story of Heathcliff, how Emily Brontë has torn and rent at her own soul in the creation of this appalling figure. Heathcliff, without father or mother, without even a Christian name, becomes for us a sort of personal embodiment of the suppressed fury of Emily Brontë's own soul. The cautious prudence and hypocritical reserves of the discreet world of timid, kindly, compromising human beings has got upon the nerves of this formidable girl, and, as she goes tearing and rending at all the masks which cover our loves and our hates, she seems to utter wild discordant cries, cries like those of some she-wolf rushing through the herd of normal human sheep.

Heathcliff and Cathy, what a pair they are! What terrifying lovers! They seem to have arisen from some remote unfathomed past of the world's earlier and less civilised passions. And yet, one occasionally catches, as one goes through the world, the Heathcliff look upon the face of a man and the Cathy look upon the face of a woman.

In a writer of less genius than Emily Brontë Heathcliff would never have found his match; would never have found his mate, his equal, his twin-soul.

It needed the imagination of one who had both Heathcliff and Cathy in her to dig them both out of the same granite rock, covered with yellow gorse and purple ling, and to hurl them into one another's arms.

From the moment when they inscribed their initials upon the walls of that melancholy room, to the moment when, with a howl like a madman, Heathcliff drags her from her grave, their affiliation is desperate and absolute.

This is a love which passes far beyond all sensuality, far beyond all voluptuous pleasure. They get little good of their love, these two—little solace and small comfort.

But one cannot conceive their wishing to change their lot with any happier lovers. They are what they are, and they are prepared to endure what fate shall send them.

When Cathy admits to the old servant that she intends to marry Linton because Heathcliff was unworthy of her and would drag her down, "I love Linton," she says—"but *I am* Heathcliff!" And this *"I am* Heathcliff" rings in our ears as the final challenge to a chaotic pluralistic world full of cynical disillusionment, of the desperate spirit of which Emily Brontë was made.

The wild madness of such love—passing the love of men and women—may seem to many readers the mere folly of an insane dream.

Emily Brontë—as she was bound to do—tosses them forth, that inhuman pair, upon the voyaging homeless wind; tosses them forth, free of their desperation, to wander at large, ghosts of their own undying passions, over the face of the rainswept moors. But to most quiet and sceptical souls such an issue of the drama contradicts the laws of nature. To most patient slaves of destiny the end of the ashes of these fierce flames is to mingle placidly with the dark earth of those misty hills and find their release in nothing more tragic than the giving to the roots of the heather and the bracken a richer soil wherein to grow.

None of us know! None of us can ever know! It is enough that in this extraordinary story the wild strange link which once and again in the history of a generation binds so strangely two persons together, almost as though their association were the result of some aeon-old everlasting Recurrence, is once more thrown into tragic relief and given the tender beauty of an austere imagination.

Not every one can feel the spell of Emily Brontë or care for her work. To some she must always remain too ungracious, too savage, too uncompromising. But for those who have come to care for her, she is a wonderful and a lovely figure; a figure whose full significance has not even yet been sounded, a figure with whom we must come more and more to associate that liberation of what we call love from the mere animalism of sexual passion, which we feel sometimes, and in our rarer moments, to be one of the richest triumphs of the spirit over the flesh.

It may be that Emily Brontë is right. It may be that a point can be reached—perhaps is already being reached in the lives of certain individuals—where sexual passion is thus surpassed and transcended by the burning of a flame more intense than any which lust can produce.

It may be that the human race, as time goes on, will follow closer and closer this ferocious and spiritual girl in tearing aside the compromises of our hesitating timidity and plunging into the ice-cold waters of passions so keen and translunar as to have become chaste. It may be so—and, on the other hand, it may be that the old sly earth-gods will hold their indelible sway over us until the "baseless fabric" of this vision leaves "not a rack behind"! In any case, for our present purpose, the reading of Emily Brontë strengthens us in our recognition that the only wisdom of life consists in leaving all the doors of the universe open.

Cursed be they who close any doors! Let that be our literary as it is our philosophical motto.

Little have we gained from books, little from our passionate following in the steps of the great masters, if, after all, we only return once more to the narrow prejudices of our obstinate personal convictions.

From ourselves we cannot escape; but we can, unfortunately, hide ourselves from ourselves. We can hide ourselves "full-fathom-five" under our convictions and our principles. We can hide ourselves under our theories and our philosophies. It is only now and again, when, by some sudden devastating flash, some terrific burst of the thunder of the great gods, the real lineaments of what we are show up clearly for a moment in the dark mirror of our shaken consciousness.

It is well not to let the memory of those moments pass altogether away.

The reading of the great authors will have been a mere epicurean pastime if it has not made us recognise that what is important in our life is something that belongs more closely to us than any opinion we have inherited or any theory we have gained or any principle we have struggled for.

It will have been wasted if it has not made us recognise that in the moments when these outward things fall away, and the true self, beyond the power of these outward things, looks forth defiantly, tenderly, pitifully upon this huge strange world, there are intimations and whispers of something beyond all that the philosophers have ever dreamed, hidden in the reservoirs of being and ready to touch us with their breath.

Our reading of these noble writings will have been no more than a gracious entertainment if we have not come to see that the enormous differences of their verdicts prove conclusively that no one theory, no one principle, can cover the tremendous field. But such reading will have had but a poor effect if because of this radical opposition in the voices reaching us we give up our interest in the great quest.

For it is upon our retaining our interest that the birthright of our humanity depends.

We shall never find what we seek; that is certain enough. We should be gods, not men, if we found it. But we should be less than men, and beasts—if we gave up the interest of the search, the tremulous vibrating interest, which, like little waves of ether, hovers over the cross-roads where all the great ways part.

Something outside ourselves drives us on to seek it—this evasive solution of a riddle that seems eternal—and when, weary with the effort of refusing this or the other premature solution, weary with the effort of suspending our judgment and standing erect at that parting of the ways, we long in our hearts to drift at leisure down one of the many soothing streams, it is only the knowledge that it is not our intrinsic inmost self that so collapses and yields up the high prerogative of doubt, but some lesser self in us, some tired superficial self, which keeps us back from that betrayal. The courage with which Emily Brontë faced life, the equanimity with which she faced death, were in her case closely associated with the quiet desolate landscape which surrounded her. As my American poet says, it is only in the country that we can look upon these fatal necessities and see them as they are. To be born and to die fall into their place when we are living where the smell of the earth can reach us.

There will always be a difference between those who come from the country and those who come from the town; and if a time ever arrives when the cities of men so cover the earth that there will be room no longer for any country-bred persons in our midst, something will in that hour pass away forever from art and literature, and, I suspect, from philosophy too.

For you cannot acquire this quality by any pleasant trips through picturesque scenery. It is either in you or it is not in you. You either have the slow, tenacious, humorous, patient, imaginative instincts of the country-born; or you have the smart, quick, clever, witty, fanciful, lively, receptive, caustic turn of mind of those bred in the great cities.

We all come to the town, "some in rags and some in jags and some in velvet gowns"; but the country-born always recognises the country-born, and there is a natural affinity between them.

I suspect that those who have behind them no local, provincial traditions will find it difficult to understand Emily Brontë.

She did not deal in elaborate description; but the earth-mould smells sweet, and the roots of the reeds of the pond-rushes show wavering and dim in the dark water, and "through the hawthorn blows the cold wind," and the white moon drifts over the sombre furze-covered hills; and all these things have passed into her style and have formed her style, and all these things are behind the tenacity with which she endures life, and behind the immense mysterious hope with which, while regarding all human creeds as "unutterably vain," she falls back so fiercely upon that "amor intellectualis Dei" which is the burning fire in her own soul.

> —"Thou, thou art being and breath;
> And what thou art can never be destroyed!"

AN EXCERPT FROM
Suspended Judgments
- Essays on Books and Sensations, 1916

CHARLOTTE
AND EMILY BRONTË

BY ALICE MEYNELL

The controversy here is with those who admire Charlotte Brontë throughout her career. She altered greatly. She did, in fact, inherit a manner of English that had been strained beyond restoration, fatigued beyond recovery, by the "corrupt following" of Gibbon; and there was within her a sense of propriety that caused her to conform. Straitened and serious elder daughter of her time, she kept the house of literature. She practised those verbs, to evince, to reside, to intimate, to peruse. She wrote "communicating instruction" for teaching; "an extensive and eligible connexion"; "a small competency"; "an establishment on the Continent"; "It operated as a barrier to further intercourse"; and of a child (with a singular unfitness with childhood) "For the toys he possesses he seems to have contracted a partiality amounting to affection." I have been already reproached for a word on Gibbon written by way of parenthesis in the course of an appreciation of some other author. Let me, therefore, repeat that I am writing of the corrupt following of that apostle and not of his own style. Gibbon's grammar is frequently weak, but the corrupt followers have something worse than poor grammar. Gibbon set the fashion of "the latter" and "the former." Our literature was for at least half a century strewn with the wreckage of Gibbon. "After suppressing a competitor who had assumed the purple at Mentz, he refused to gratify his troops with the plunder of the rebellious city," writes the great historian. When Mr. Micawber confesses "gratifying emotions of no common description" he conforms to a lofty and a distant Gibbon. So does Mr. Pecksniff when he says of the copper-founder's daughter that she "has shed a vision on my path refulgent in its nature." And when an author, in a work on "The Divine Comedy," recently told us that Paolo and Francesca were to receive from Dante "such alleviation as circumstances would allow," that also is a shattered, a waste Gibbon, a waif of Gibbon. For Johnson less than Gibbon inflated the English our fathers inherited; because Johnson did not habitually or often use imagery, whereas Gibbon did use habitual imagery, and such use is what deprives a language of elasticity, and leaves it either rigid or languid, oftener languid. Encumbered by this drift and refuse of English, Charlotte Brontë yet achieved the miracle of her vocabulary. It is less wonderful that she should have appeared out of such a parsonage than that she should have arisen out of such a language.

A re-reading of her works is always a new amazing of her reader who turns back to review the harvest of her English. It must have been with rapture that she claimed her own simplicity. And with what a moderation, how temperately, and how seldom she used her mastery! To the last she has an occasional attachment to her bonds; for she was not only fire and air. In one passage of her life she may remind us of the little colourless and thrifty hen-bird that Lowell watched nest-building with her mate, and cutting short the flutterings and billings wherewith he would joyously interrupt the business; Charlotte's nesting bird was a clergyman. He came, lately affianced, for a week's visit to her parsonage, and she wrote to her friend before his arrival: "My little plans have been disarranged by an intimation that Mr.—is coming on Monday"; and afterwards, in reference to her sewing, "he hindered me for a full week."

In alternate pages *Villette* is a book of spirit and fire, and a novel of illiberal rancour, of ungenerous, uneducated anger, ungentle, ignoble. In order to forgive its offences, we have to remember in its author's favour not her pure style set free, not her splendour in literature, but rather the immeasurable sorrow of her life. To read of that sorrow again is to open once more a wound which most men perhaps, certainly most women, received into their hearts in childhood. For the Life of Charlotte Brontë is one of the first books of biography put into the hands of a child, to whom *Jane Eyre* is allowed only in passages. We are young when we first hear in what narrow beds "the three are laid"—the two sisters and the brother—and in what a bed of living insufferable memories the one left lay alone, reviewing the hours of their death—alone in the sealed house that was only less narrow than their graves. The rich may set apart and dedicate a room, the poor change their street, but Charlotte Brontë, in the close captivity of the fortunes of mediocrity, rested in the chair that had been her dying sister's, and held her melancholy bridals in the dining room that had been the scene of terrible and reluctant death.

But closer than the conscious house was the conscious mind. Locked with intricate wards within the unrelaxing and unlapsing thoughts of this lonely sister, dwelt a sorrow inconsolable. It is well for the perpetual fellowship of mankind that no child should read this life and not take therefrom a perdurable scar, albeit her heart was somewhat frigid towards childhood, and she died before her motherhood could be born.

Mistress of some of the best prose of her century, Charlotte Brontë was subject to a Lewes, a Chorley, a Miss Martineau: that is, she suffered what in Italian is called *soggezione* in their presence. When she had met six minor contemporary writers— by-products of literature—at dinner, she had a headache and a sleepless night. She writes to her friend that these contributors to the quarterly press are greatly feared in literary London, and there is in her letter a sense of tremor and exhaustion. And what nights did the heads of the critics undergo after the meeting? Lewes, whose own romances are all condoned, all forgiven by time and oblivion, who gave her lessons, who told her to study Jane Austen? The others, whose reviews doubtless did their proportionate part in still further hunting and harrying the tired English of their day? And before Harriet Martineau she bore herself reverently. Harriet Martineau, albeit a woman of masculine understanding (we may imagine we hear her contemporaries give her the title), could not thread her way safely in and out of two or three negatives, but wrote—about this very Charlotte Brontë: "I did not consider the book a coarse one, though I could not answer for it that there were no traits which, on a second leisurely reading, I might not dislike." Mrs. Gaskell quotes the passage with no consciousness of anything amiss.

As for Lewes's vanished lesson upon the methods of Jane Austen, it served one only sufficient purpose. Itself is not quoted by anyone alive, but Charlotte Brontë's rejoinder adds one to our little treasury of her incomparable pages. If they were twenty, they are twenty-one by the addition of this, written in a long-neglected letter and saved for us by Mr. Shorter's research, for I believe his is the only record: "What sees keenly, speaks aptly, moves flexibly, it suits her to study; but what throbs fast and full, though hidden, what blood rushes through, what is the unseen seat of life and the sentient target of death—that Miss Austen ignores."

When the author of *Jane Eyre* faltered before six authors, more or less, at dinner in London, was it the writer of her second-class English who was shy? or was it the author of the passages here to follow?—and therefore one for whom the national tongue was much the better? There can be little doubt. The Charlotte Brontë who used the English of a world long corrupted by "one good custom"—the good custom of Gibbon's Latinity grown fatally popular—could at any time hold up her head amongst her reviewers; for her there was no sensitive interior solitude in that society. She who cowered was the Charlotte who made Rochester recall "the simple yet sagacious grace" of Jane's first smile; she who wrote: "I looked at my love; it shivered in my heart like a suffering child in a cold cradle"; who wrote: "To see what a heavy lid day slowly lifted, what a wan glance she flung upon the hills, you would have thought the sun's fire quenched in last night's floods." This new genius was solitary and afraid, and touched to the quick by the eyes and voice of judges. In her worse style there was no "quick." Latin-English, whether scholarly or unscholarly, is the mediate tongue. An unscholarly Latin-English is proof against the world. The scholarly Latin-English wherefrom it is disastrously derived is, in its own nobler measure, a defence against more august assaults than those of criticism. In the strength of it did Johnson hold parley with his profounder sorrows—hold parley (by his phrase), make terms (by his definition), give them at last lodging and entertainment after sentence and treaty.

And the meaner office of protection against reviewers and the world was doubtless done by the meaner Latinity. The author of the phrase "The child contracted a partiality for his toys" had no need to fear any authors she might meet at dinner. Against Charlotte Brontë's sorrows her worse manner of English never stands for a moment. Those vain phrases fall from before her face and her bared heart. To the heart, to the heart she took the shafts of her griefs. She tells them therefore as she suffered them, vitally and mortally. "A great change approached. Affliction came in that shape which to anticipate is dread; to look back on, grief. My sister Emily first declined. Never in all her life had she lingered over any task that lay before her, and she did not linger now. She made haste to leave us." "I remembered where the three were laid—in what narrow, dark dwellings." "Do you know this place? No, you never saw it; but you recognize the nature of these trees, this foliage—the cypress, the willow, the yew. Stone crosses like these are not unfamiliar to you, nor are these dim garlands of everlasting flowers. Here is the place." "Then the watcher approaches the patient's pillow, and sees a new and strange moulding of the familiar features, feels at once that the insufferable moment draws nigh." In the same passage comes another single word of genius, "the sound that so wastes our strength." And, fine as "wastes," is the "wronged" of another sentence—"some wronged and fettered wild beast or bird."

It is easy to gather such words, more difficult to separate the best from such a mingled page as that on "Imagination": "A spirit, softer and better than human reason, had descended with quiet flight to the waste"; and "My hunger has this good angel appeased with food sweet and strange"; and "This daughter of Heaven remembered me to-night; she saw me weep, and she came with comfort; 'Sleep,' she said, 'sleep sweetly—I gild thy dreams.'" "Was this feeling dead? I do not know, but it was buried. Sometimes I thought the tomb unquiet."

Perhaps the most "eloquent" pages are unluckily those wherein we miss the friction—friction of water to the oar, friction of air to the pinion—friction that sensibly proves the use, the buoyancy, the act of language. Sometimes an easy eloquence resembles the easy labours of the daughters of Danaus. To draw water in a sieve is an easy art, rapid and relaxed.

But no laxity is ever, I think, to be found in her brief passages of landscape. "The keen, still cold of the morning was succeeded, later in the day, by a sharp breathing from the Russian wastes; the cold zone sighed over the temperate zone and froze it fast." "Not till the destroying angel of tempest had achieved his perfect work would he fold the wings whose waft was thunder, the tremor of whose plumes was storm." "The night is not calm: the equinox still struggles in its storms. The wild rains of the day are abated: the great single cloud disappears and rolls away from Heaven, not passing and leaving a sea all sapphire, but tossed buoyant before a continued, long-sounding, high-rushing moonlight tempest. . . No Endymion will watch for his goddess to-night: there are no flocks on the mountains." See, too, this ocean: "The sway of the whole Great Deep above a herd of whales rushing through the livid and liquid thunder down from the frozen zone." And this promise of the visionary Shirley: "I am to be walking by myself on deck, rather late of an August evening, watching and being watched by a full harvest moon: something is to rise white on the surface of the sea, over which that moon mounts silent, and hangs glorious. . . I think I hear it cry with an articulate voice. .

. . I show you an image fair as alabaster emerging from the dim wave."

Charlotte Brontë knew well the experience of dreams. She seems to have undergone the inevitable dream of mourners—the human dream of the Labyrinth, shall I call it? the uncertain spiritual journey in search of the waiting and sequestered dead, which is the obscure subject of the "Eurydice" of Coventry Patmore's Odes. There is the lately dead, in exile, remote, betrayed, foreign, indifferent, sad, forsaken by some vague malice or neglect, sought by troubled love astray.

In Charlotte Brontë's page there is an autumnal and tempestuous dream. "A nameless experience that had the hue, the mien, the terror, the very tone of a visitation from eternity. . . Suffering brewed in temporal or calculable measure tastes not as this suffering tasted." Finally, is there any need to cite the passage of *Jane Eyre* that contains the avowal, the vigil in the garden? Those are not words to be forgotten. Some tell you that a fine style will give you the memory of a scene and not of the recording words that are the author's means. And others again would have the phrase to be remembered foremost. Here, then, in *Jane Eyre*, are both memories equal. The night is perceived, the phrase is an experience; both have their place in the reader's irrevocable past. "Custom intervened between me and what I naturally and inevitably loved." "Jane, do you hear that nightingale singing in the wood?" "A waft of wind came sweeping down the laurel walk, and trembled through the boughs of the chestnut; it wandered away to an infinite distance. . . The nightingale's voice was then the only voice of the hour; in listening I again wept."

* * * * *

Whereas Charlotte Brontë walked, with exultation and enterprise, upon the road of symbols, under the guidance of her own visiting genius, Emily seldom went out upon those far avenues. She was one who practised imagery sparingly. Her style had the key of an inner prose which seems to leave imagery behind in the way of approaches—the apparelled and arrayed approaches and ritual of literature—and so to go further and to be admitted among simple realities and antitypes.

Charlotte Brontë also knew that simple goal, but she loved her imagery. In the passage of *Jane Eyre* that tells of the return to Thornfield Hall, in ruins by fire, she bespeaks her reader's romantic attention to an image which in truth is not all golden. She has moments, on the other hand, of pure narrative, whereof each word is such a key as I spoke of but now, and unlocks an inner and an inner plain door of spiritual realities. There is, perhaps, no author who, simply telling what happened, tells it with so great a significance: "Jane, did you hear that nightingale singing in the wood?" and "She made haste to leave us." But her characteristic calling is to images, those avenues and temples oracular, and to the vision of symbols.

You may hear the poet of great imagery praised as a great mystic. Nevertheless, although a great mystical poet makes images, he does not do so in his greatest moments. He is a great mystic, because he has a full vision of the mystery of realities, not because he has a clear invention of similitudes.

Of many thousand kisses the poor last,

and

Now with his love, now in the colde grave

are lines on the yonder side of imagery. So is this line also:

Sad with the promise of a different sun,

and

> Piteous passion keen at having found,
> After exceeding ill, a little good.

Shakespeare, Chaucer and Patmore yield us these great examples. Imagery is for the time when, as in these lines, the shock of feeling (which must needs pass, as the heart beats and pauses) is gone by:

> Thy heart with dead winged innocence filled,
> Even as a nest with birds,
> After the old ones by the hawk are killed.

I cite these lines of Patmore's because of their imagery in a poem that without them would be insupportably close to spiritual facts; and because it seems to prove with what a yielding hand at play the poet of realities holds his symbols for a while. A great writer is both a major and a minor mystic, in the self-same poem; now suddenly close to his mystery (which is his greater moment) and anon making it mysterious with imagery (which is the moment of his most beautiful lines).

The student passes delighted through the several courts of poetry, from the outer to the inner, from riches to more imaginative riches, and from decoration to more complex decoration; and prepares himself for the greater opulence of the innermost chamber. But when he crosses the last threshold he finds this mid-most sanctuary to be a hypaethral temple, and in its custody and care a simple earth and a space of sky.

Emily Brontë seems to have a nearly unparalleled unconsciousness of the delays, the charms, the pauses and preparations of imagery. Her strength does not dally with the parenthesis, and her simplicity is ignorant of those rites. Her lesser work, therefore, is plain narrative, and her greater work is no more. On the hither side—the daily side—of imagery she is still a strong and solitary writer; on the yonder side she has written some of the most mysterious passages in all plain prose.

And with what direct and incommunicable art! "'Let me alone, let me alone,' said Catherine. 'If I've done wrong, I'm dying for it. You left me too . . . I forgive you. Forgive me!' 'It is hard to forgive, and to look at those eyes and feel those wasted hands,' he answered. 'Kiss me again, and don't let me see your eyes! I forgive what you have done to me. I love my murderer—but *yours*! How can I?' They were silent, their faces hid against each other, and washed by each other's tears." "So much the worse for me that I am strong," cries Heathcliff in the same scene. "Do I want to live? What kind of living will it be when you—Oh God, would you like to live with your soul in the grave?"

Charlotte Brontë's noblest passages are her own speech or the speech of one like herself acting the central part in the dreams and dramas of emotion that she had kept from her girlhood—the unavowed custom of the ordinary girl by her so splendidly avowed in a confidence that comprised the world. Emily had no such confessions to publish. She contrived—but the word does not befit her singular spirit of liberty, that knew nothing of stealth—to remove herself from the world; as her person left no pen-portrait, so her "I" is not heard here. She lends her voice in disguise to her men and women; the first narrator of her great romance is a young man, the second a servant woman; this one or that among the actors takes up the story, and her great words sound at times in paltry mouths. It is then that for a moment her reader seems about to come into her immediate presence, but by a fiction she denies herself to him. To a somewhat trivial girl (or a girl who would be trivial in any other book, but Emily Brontë seems unable to create anything consistently meagre)—to Isabella Linton she commits one of her most memorable passages, and one which has the rare image, one of a terrifying little company of visions amid terrifying facts: "His attention was roused, I saw, for his eyes rained down tears among the ashes. . . The clouded windows of hell flashed for a moment towards me; the fiend which usually looked out was so dimmed and drowned." But in Heathcliff's own speech there is no veil or circumstance. "I'm too happy; and yet I'm not happy enough. My soul's bliss kills my body, but does not satisfy itself." "I have to remind myself to breathe, and almost to remind my heart to beat." "Being alone, and conscious two yards of loose earth was the sole barrier between us, I said to myself: 'I'll have her in my arms again.' If she be cold, I'll think it is this north wind that chills me; and if she be motionless, it is sleep." What art, moreover, what knowledge, what a fresh ear for the clash of repetition; what a chime in that phrase: "I dreamt I was sleeping the last sleep by that sleeper, with my heart stopped, and my cheek frozen against hers."

Emily Brontë was no student of books. It was not from among the fruits of any other author's labour that she gathered these eminent words. But I think I have found the suggestion of this action of Heathcliff's—the disinterment. Not in any inspiring ancient Irish legend, as has been suggested, did Emily Brontë find her incident; she found it (but she made, and did not find, its beauty) in a mere costume romance of Bulwer Lytton, whom Charlotte Brontë, as we know, did not admire. And Emily showed no sign at all of admiration when she did him so much honour as to borrow the action of his studio-bravo.

Heathcliff's love for Catherine's past childhood is one of the profound surprises of this unparalleled book; it is to call her childish ghost—the ghost of the little girl—when she has been a dead adult woman twenty years that the inhuman lover opens the window of the house on the Heights. Something is this that the reader knew not how to look for. Another thing known to genius and beyond a reader's hope is the tempestuous purity of those passions. This wild quality of purity has a counterpart in the brief passages of nature that make the summers, the waters, the woods, and the windy heights of that murderous story seem so sweet. The "beck" that was audible beyond the hills after rain, the "heath on the top of Wuthering Heights" whereon, in her dream of Heaven, Catherine, flung out by angry angels, awoke sobbing for joy; the bird whose feathers she—delirious creature—plucks from the pillow of her deathbed ("This—I should know it among a thousand—it's a lapwing's. Bonny bird; wheeling over our heads in the middle of the moor. It wanted to get to its nest, for the clouds had touched the swells and it felt rain coming"); the only two white spots of snow left on all the moors, and the brooks brim-full; the old apple-trees, the smell of stocks and wallflowers in the brief summer, the few fir-trees by Catherine's window-bars, the early moon—I know not where are landscapes more exquisite and natural. And among the signs of death where is any fresher than the window seen from the garden to be swinging open in the morning, when Heathcliff lay within, dead and drenched with rain?

None of these things are presented by images. Nor is that signal passage wherewith the book comes to a close. Be it permitted to cite it here again. It has taken its place, it is among the paragons of our literature. Our language will not lapse or derogate while this prose stands for appeal: "I lingered . . . under that benign sky; watched the moths fluttering among the heath and harebells, listened to the soft wind breathing through the grass, and wondered how anyone could ever imagine unquiet slumbers for the sleepers in that quiet earth."

Finally, of Emily Brontë's face the world holds only an obviously unskilled reflection, and of her aspect no record worth having. Wild fugitive, she vanished, she escaped, she broke away, exiled by the neglect of her contemporaries, banished by their disrespect outlawed by their contempt, dismissed by their indifference. And such an one was she as might rather have pronounced upon these the sentence passed by Coriolanus under sentence of expulsion; she might have driven the world from before her face and cast it out from her presence as he condemned his Romans: "*I* banish you."

An Excerpt From
Hearts of Controversy , 1918

THE CHALLENGE OF THE BRONTËS

BY EDMUND WILLIAM GOSSE

Although I possess in no degree the advantage which so many of the members of your society enjoy in being personally connected with the scenes and even, perhaps, with the characters associated with the Brontë family, I cannot begin my little address to you to-day without some invocation of the genius of the place. We meet at Dewsbury because the immortal sisters were identified with Dewsbury. Is it then not imperative that for whatever picture of them I may endeavour to present before you this afternoon, Dewsbury should form the background? Unfortunately, however, although in the hands of a skilful painter the figures of the ladies may glow forth, I fear that in the matter of taking Dewsbury as the background some vagueness and some darkness are inevitable. In the biographies of Mrs. Gaskell and of Mr. Clement Shorter, as well as in the proceedings of your society, I have searched for evidences of the place Dewsbury took in the lives of the Brontës. What I find—I expect you to tell me that it is not exhaustive—is this. Their father, the Rev. Patrick Brontë, was curate here from 1809 to 1811. In 1836, when Charlotte was twenty, Miss Wooler transferred her school from Roe Head to Heald's House at the top of Dewsbury Moor. In this school, where Charlotte had been a pupil since 1831, she was now a governess, and a governess she remained until early in 1838. In April of that year Miss Wooler was taken ill and Charlotte was for a little while in charge. Then there was an explosion of temper, of some kind, and Charlotte went back to Haworth.

That, then, in the main, is the limit of what the scrupulous Muse of history vouchsafes to tell us about Charlotte Brontë's relation to Dewsbury. But it also supplies us with one or two phrases which I cannot bring myself to spare you. In January 1838, Charlotte reviews her experience at Dewsbury Moor; "I feel," she says, "in nothing better, nothing humbler nor purer." Again, in 1841, after there had passed time enough to mellow her exacerbations, she continues to express herself with vigour. Miss Wooler is making overtures to Charlotte and Emily to take over the school at Heald's House; perhaps a place might be found for Anne as well. Miss Wooler, one of the kindest of women, is most thoughtful, most conciliatory. Charlotte will have none of the idea; she puts it roughly from her. Of Dewsbury she has nothing to say but that "it is a poisoned place for me." This is all we know of Charlotte's relation to Dewsbury, yet nothing, you will tell me, in Froude's phrase, to what the angels know. Well, I must be frank with you and say that I am afraid the angels have been inclined to record exceedingly little of Charlotte Brontë's residence in your inoffensive neighbourhood. I have to paint a background to my picture, and I find none but the gloomiest colours. They have to be what the art-critics of the eighteenth century called "sub-fusc." But it is not the fault of Dewsbury, it is the fault, or the misfortune, of our remarkable little genius. She was here, in this wholesome and hospitable vicinity, for several months, during which time "she felt in nothing better, neither humbler nor purer," and looking back upon it, she had to admit that it was "a poisoned place" to her.

I cannot help fancying that you will agree with me, that on such an occasion as the present, and especially when dealing with a group of writers about whom so much as has been said as about the Brontës, it is wise not to cover too wide a ground, but to take, and keep to, one aspect of the subject. Our little excursion into the history seems to have given us, under the heading "Dewsbury," a rather grim text, from which, nevertheless, we may perhaps extract some final consolation. Let me say at the outset that for the grimness, for the harshness, Dewsbury is not at all to blame. I fancy that if, in the years from 1836 to 1838, the Brontë girls had been visitors to Kubla Khan, and had been fed on honey by his myrmidons at Xanadu, that pleasure-dome would yet have been "poisoned" to them. It was not poverty, and cold, and the disagreeable position of a governess, it was not the rough landscape of your moors, nor its lack of southern amenity which made Charlotte wretched here. It was not in good Miss Wooler, nor in the pupils, nor in the visitors at Heald's House that the mischief lay, it was in the closed and patient crater of Charlotte's own bosom. And I am almost persuaded that, if you had lived in Dewsbury sixty-five years ago, you would have heard on very quiet days a faint subterranean sound which you would never have been able to guess was really the passion, furiously panting, shut up in the heart of a small, pale governess in Heald's House schoolroom.

If you accuse me of fatalism, I am helpless in your hands, for I confess I do not see how it could be otherwise, and do scarcely wish that it could have been. Let us not be too sentimental in this matter. Figures in literature are notable and valuable to us for what they give us. The more personal and intense and definite that is, the greater the gift, the more strenuous the toil and the more severe the initiation which lead to its expression. The Brontës had a certain thing to learn to give; what that was we shall presently try to note. But whatever we find it to be, we start with allowing that it was extremely and boldly original. It was not to be mastered by lying upon padded sofas and toying with a little Berlin wool-work. It involved pain, resistance, a stern revision of things hitherto taken for granted. The secrets which they designed to wring from nature and from life were not likely to be revealed to the self-indulgent and the dilettante. The sisters had a message from the sphere of indignation and revolt. In order that they should learn it as well as teach it, it was necessary that they should arrive on the scene at an evil hour for their own happiness. *Jane Eyre* and *Shirley* and *Villette* could not have been written unless, for long years, the world had been "a poisoned place" for Charlotte Brontë.

It has been excellently said by Mrs. Humphry Ward that in many respects, and to the very last, the Brontës challenge no less than they attract us. This is an aspect which, in the midst of rapturous modern heroine-worship, we are apt to forget. Thackeray, who respected the genius of the family, and was immensely kind to the author of *Jane Eyre*, never really felt comfortable in her company. We know how he stole out of his own front-door, and slipped away into the night to escape her. "A very austere little person," he called her, and we may put what emphasis on the austerity we will. I feel sure that any maladroit "white-washing of Charlotte" will tend, sooner or later, good-natured though it may be, in a failure to comprehend what she really was, in what her merit consisted, what the element in her was that, for instance, calls us here together nearly half a century after she completed her work and passed away. Young persons of genius very commonly write depressing books; since, the more vivid an unripe creature's impression of life is, the more acute is its distress. It is only extremely stupid Sunday-school children who shout in chorus, "We are so happy, happy, happy!" Genius thrown naked, with exposed nerves, on a hard indifferent world, is never "happy" at first. Earth is a "poisoned place" to it, until it has won its way and woven its garments and discovered its food.

But in the case of Charlotte Brontë, unhappiness was more than juvenile fretfulness. All her career was a revolt against conventionality, against isolation, against irresistible natural forces, such as climate and ill-health and physical insignificance. Would this insubmissive spirit have passed out of her writings, as it passed, for instance, out of those of George Sand? I am not sure, for we see it as strongly, though more gracefully and skilfully expressed, in *Villette* as in the early letters which her biographers have printed. Her hatred of what was commonplace and narrow and obvious flung her against a wall of prejudice, which she could not break down. She could only point to it by her exhausting efforts; she could only invite the generation which succeeded her to bring their pickaxes to bear upon it. Hence, to the very last, she seems, more than any other figure in our literature, to be forever ruffled in temper, for ever angry and wounded and indignant, rejecting consolation, crouched like a sick animal in the cavern of her own quenchless pride. This is not an amiable attitude, nor is it historically true that this was Charlotte Brontë's constant aspect. But I will venture to say that her amiabilities, her yielding moods, are really the unessential parts of her disposition, and that a certain admirable ferocity is the notable feature of her intellectual character.

Her great heart was always bleeding. Here at Dewsbury, in the years we are contemplating, the hemorrhage was of the most doleful kind, for it was concealed, suppressed, it was an inward flow. When once she became an author the pain of her soul was relieved. She said, in 1850, looking back on the publication of the hapless first volume of poems, "The mere effort to succeed gave a wonderful zest to existence." Then, a little later, when no one had paid the slightest attention to the slender trio of maiden voices, "Something like the chill of despair began to invade their hearts." With a less powerful inspiration, they must have ceased to make the effort; they must have succumbed in a melancholy oblivion. But they were saved by the instinct of a mission. It was not their private grief which primarily stirred them. What urged them on was the dim consciousness that they gave voice to a dumb sense of the suffering of all the world. They had to go on working; they had to pursue their course, though it might seem sinister or fatal; their business was to move mankind, not to indulge or please it. They "must be honest; they must not varnish, soften, or conceal."

What Charlotte Brontë was learning to do in her grim and, let us admit it, her unlovely probation on Dewsbury Moor, was to introduce a fresh aspect of the relations of literature to life. Every great writer has a new note; hers was—defiance. All the aspects in which life presented itself to her were distressing, not so much in themselves as in herself. She rebelled against the outrages of poverty, and she drank to its dregs the cup of straitened circumstances. She was proud, as proud as Lucifer, and she was forced into positions which suppleness and cheerfulness might have made tolerable, if not agreeable. She wrung from these positions their last drop of bitterness. A very remarkable instance of this may be found in her relation to the Sidgwick family, who, by universal report, were generous, genial, and unassuming. To Charlotte Brontë these kindly, if somewhat commonplace folk, grew to seem what a Turkish pasha seems to the inhabitants of a Macedonian village. It was not merely the surroundings of her life—it was life itself, in its general mundane arrangements, which was intolerable to her. She fretted in it, she beat her wings against its bars, and she would have done the same if those bars had been of gold, and if the fruits of paradise had been pushed to her between them. This, I think, is why the expression of her anger seems too often disproportionate, and why her irony is so apt to be preposterous. She was born to resist being caged in any form. Her defiance was universal, and often it was almost indiscriminate.

Do not let us presume to blame this insubmission. Still less let us commit the folly of minimising it. A good cheerful little Charlotte Brontë, who thought the best of everybody, who gaily took her place without a grudging sigh, whose first aim was to make those about her happy and to minister to their illusions, would have been a much more welcome inmate of Miss Wooler's household than the cantankerous governess whom nobody could please, whose susceptibilities were always on edge, whose lonely arrogance made her feared by all but one or two who timidly persisted in loving her. But such a paragon of the obvious virtues would have passed as the birds pass and as the flowers. She would have left no mark behind. She would never have enriched the literature of England by one of its master-evidences of the force of human will. She would never have stirred hundreds of thousands of consciences to a wholesome questioning of fate and their own souls.

Let us endeavour to pursue the inquiry a few steps further. It is impossible to separate the ethical conditions of an author's mind from the work that he produces. The flower requires the soil; it betrays in its colour and its perfume the environment of its root. The moral constitution of the writer is reflected in the influence of the written page. This is the incessant contention; on one hand the independence of art asserts itself; on the other, it is impossible to escape from the implicit influence of conduct upon art. There have been few writers of any age in whom this battle raged more fiercely than it did in Charlotte Brontë. Her books, and those of her sisters, seem anodyne enough to-day; to readers of a sensitive species they seemed, when they were published, as dangerous as *Werther* had been, as seductive as the *Nouvelle Heloïse*. The reason of this was, in the main, the spirit of revolt which inspired them. There was something harsh and glaring in their landscape; there was that touch of Salvator Rosa which one of their earliest critics observed in them. But more essential was the stubbornness, the unflinching determination to revise all accepted formulas of conduct, to do this or that, not because it was usual to do it, but because it was rational, and in harmony with human nature.

Into an age which had become almost exclusively utilitarian, and in which the exercise of the imagination, in its real forms, was sedulously discountenanced, Charlotte Brontë introduced passion in the sphere of prose fiction, as Byron had introduced it in the sphere of verse thirty years earlier. It was an inestimable gift; it had to come to us, from Charlotte Brontë or another, to save our literature from a decline into triviality and pretension. But she suffered, as Byron had suffered, in the direct ratio of her originality. If a writer employs passion in an age which has ceased to recognise it as one of the necessities of literary vitality he is safe to be accused of perverting his readers. Balzac says, "When nothing else can be charged against an author, the reproach of immorality is thrown at his head." When we study the record of the grim life of the sisters at Haworth, like that of three young soldiers round a camp-fire with the unseen enemy prowling in the darkness just out of their sight—when we think of the strenuous vigil, the intractable and indomitable persistence, the splendour of the artistic result—we may console ourselves in our anger at the insults they endured, by reflecting how little they cared. And their noble indifference to opinion further endears them to us. We may repeat of them all what Charlotte in a letter once said of Emily, "A certain harshness in her powerful and peculiar character only makes me cling to her more."

This insubmissiveness, which was the unconscious armour given to protect her against the inevitable attacks of fortune, while, on the other hand, it was the very sign-manual of Charlotte's genius, was, on the other, a drawback from which she did not live long enough to emancipate her nature. It is responsible for her lack of interest in what is delicate and complex; it excused to herself a narrowness of vision which we are sometimes tempted to find quite distressing. It is probably the cause of a fault that never quits her for long, a tendency to make her characters express themselves with a lyrical extravagance which sometimes comes close to the confines of rodomontade. Charlotte Brontë never arrives at that mastery of her material which permits the writer to stand apart from his work, and sway the reader with successive tides of emotion while remaining perfectly calm himself. Nor is she one of those whose visible emotion is nevertheless fugitive, like an odour, and evaporates, leaving behind it works of art which betray no personal agitation. On the contrary, her revolt, her passion, all the violence of her sensibility, are present on her written page, and we cannot read it with serenity or with a merely captious curiosity, because her own eager spirit, immortal in its active force, seems to throb beside it.

The aspect of Charlotte Brontë which I have tried to indicate to you to-day, and which I have sketched thus hastily and slightly against the background of her almost voiceless residence in Dewsbury, is far from being a complete or unique one. I offer it to you only as a single facet of her wonderful temperament, of the rich spectacle of her talent. I have ventured to propose it, because, in the multiplication of honours and attentions, the tendency to deify the human, to remove those phenomena of irregularity which are the evidence of mortal strength, grows irresistible, and we find ourselves, unconsciously, substituting a waxen bust, with azure eyes and golden hair, for the homely features which (if we could but admit it) so infinitely better match the honest stories. Let us not busy ourselves to make excuse for our austere little genius of the moors. Let us be content to take her exactly as she was, with her rebellion and her narrowness, her angers and her urgencies, perceiving that she had to be this sorrowful offspring of a poisoned world in order to clear the wells of feeling for others, and to win from emancipated generations of free souls the gratitude which is due to a precursor.

AN EXCERPT FROM
Some Diversions of a Man of Letters, 1916

www.ingramcontent.com/pod-product-compliance
Lightning Source LLC
Chambersburg PA
CBHW030827090426
42737CB00009B/908